PRAISE FOR

THE SUSTAINABLE EDGE

"Ron's own personal experience on balancing family life and building wildly successful businesses provides the inspiration and real-life application that will make *The Sustainable Edge* a must read for anyone struggling with the question, 'How can I have it all?'"

—**Suzanne Siracuse**, VP/Publisher, InvestmentNews

"I've worked with Ron for more than 10 years—he's a true visionary. He lives what he preaches and has set the bar for the rest of the industry as a result. His success is inspiring, and financial professionals in every stage of their career would benefit from taking his advice and reading the life lessons shared in *The Sustainable Edge*."

—**Edmond Walters**, Founder and CEO of eMoney Advisor, LLC

"Ron Carson once again delivers valuable insights to his readers. However, the lessons shared in *The Sustainable Edge* may be the most valuable yet. Living a balanced life is simply said and difficult to achieve. Ron Carson and Scott Ford simplify this goal and provide tools you can use to lead a meaningful life."

—**Steven D. Lockshin**, Principal, AdvicePeriod

"I have benefited greatly from Ron's insight on advisor's practices over our 25-year history. He can do for you what he does for me—raise the bar on getting to top performance and strategy. If you are ready to move forward, I strongly recommend you to move your practice upward by reading this book."

—**Mark Casady**, CEO, LPL Financial

"I've witnessed Ron speak, and just like an athletic coach, I watched the advisors take the information and inspiration from his talk to help each one of them accelerate their ability to achieve success."

—**Joe Buck**, American Sportscaster

"I've known Ron for several years and seen advisors that he's worked with put these ideas into action with great success. There is a big difference between theory and practice as Ron has demonstrated in *The Sustainable Edge*."

—**Tom Nally, President**, TD Ameritrade Institutional

The

SUSTAINABLE EDGE

15 MINUTES A WEEK TO A RICHER
ENTREPRENEURIAL LIFE

New York Times Bestselling Author

RON CARSON & SCOTT FORD

GREENLEAF
BOOK GROUP PRESS

Published by Greenleaf Book Group Press
Austin, Texas
www.gbgpress.com

Distributed by Greenleaf Book Group

For ordering information or special discounts for bulk purchases, please contact Greenleaf Book Group at PO Box 91869, Austin, TX 78709, 512-891-6100.

Design and composition by Greenleaf Book Group
Cover design by Greenleaf Book Group
For permission to reprint copyrighted material, grateful acknowledgment is made to the following:
Reprinted with permission. "The Dash" by Linda Ellis.
Copyright © 1996 Linda Ellis. www.lindaellis.net.

Publisher's Cataloging-in-Publication Data is available.

ISBN: 978-1-62634-214-9

Part of the Tree Neutral® program, which offsets the number of trees consumed in the production and printing of this book by taking proactive steps, such as planting trees in direct proportion to the number of trees used: www.treeneutral.com

TreeNeutral

Printed in the United States of America on acid-free paper

15 16 17 18 19 20   10 9 8 7 6 5 4 3 2

First Edition

Other Edition(s):
eBook ISBN: 978-1-62634-215-6

I'd like to dedicate this book to The Dream
Weaver Foundation (thedreamweaverfoundation.org).
This foundation is something that I'm truly passionate about.
Jeanie and I are excited about the "Dreams" that we are granting
for the elderly who are impoverished and terminally ill. It's
our time to give back to those who have given so much.

—Ron Carson

I dedicate this book to my father who passed away in
August 2014. You instilled many of the lessons I share in
this book—like hard work, fighting for what is right, and
having a positive and optimistic attitude. Thank You.

—Scott Ford

CONTENTS

FOREWORD

Wisdom, courage, and dignity are the underlying ingredients that comprise the compelling attributes of Ron Carson and Scott Ford in both their personal and professional lives. Embarking on an effort to provide us with meaningful insight at a critical inflection point is both admirable and exceedingly important.

The Sustainable Edge introduces the combination of the most significant aspects of business and personal success. Having an edge is all well and good, but in the absence of being sustainable, it merely denotes a footnote in the transitory course of events. Sustainability without a direct link to a distinctive edge is a net consumer of energy and effort lacking a sound purpose. Delivering a pathway, based on hard-earned experience, that connects us authentically to our highest and best use is the profound reality contained within this book that translates into exceptional business performance as well as a meaningful life.

The intersection of technology, business, and personal activities has upped the ante dramatically in the need to understand what matters most and why. Good intentions alone will not crack the code of how to deal with the continuous tsunami of distractions present in today's world. A carefully constructed plan that combines genuine insight into the human condition, while effectively harnessing the power of technology to quickly filter and categorize information, is at the heart of *The Sustainable Edge*'s message.

It is with profound inspiration and gratitude that I have been able to observe firsthand the benefits and results delivered by Ron and Scott. The contagious nature of their desire to learn, grow, and develop in all aspects of their lives jumps to the forefront of any contact with them and leaves a lasting impression that is only quenched by subsequent meetings! *The Sustainable Edge* is essentially the transcribing of their DNA onto the written page.

Aristotle once said, "We are what we repeatedly do. Excellence, then, is not an act, but a habit." In each generation we must find our own relationship to the legacy we create and the willingness to strive for that higher purpose born of bold vulnerability, confidence to share, and openness to learn from others. *The Sustainable Edge* provides direct access to the repeatable excellence that can transform your life and confirm the legacy that you seek.

Robert J. Moore
March 2015
Solana Beach, California

PREFACE

A s Ron arrived in Minnesota to meet with a long-time client who had just achieved his ultimate life's goal of selling his company, he looked forward to hearing tales of high-stakes deals. At seventy three, this client had just sold his real estate development firm in Minneapolis for $174 million and had scheduled a meeting with Ron to discuss how to invest the proceeds of the sale. Ron was surprised when his client, who had pulled up to the local municipal airport in his well-used pick-up truck, seemed depressed and unsettled.

"I always thought this would be the happiest day of my life," his client said. "I messed up. I'm divorced. I have a daughter I'm not that close to. I really don't have any close friends—my friends were all work associates. My health isn't great. My whole life was about the pursuit of *more*. I worked fifteen-hour days to get ahead. The truth is, I had enough years ago."

His client's story shook Ron to his core. As business owners, we naturally want to help our entrepreneurial clients build their assets—but that is not an end in itself. If we have done our jobs well, they will be free to enjoy what makes life meaningful—faith, family, friends, community, good health, or whatever else really matters to them. His client's comments were a painful reminder of how many business leaders achieve their professional goals at the expense of their quality of life. And it's not only crazy-busy, hair-on-fire entre-preneurs who miss out on really enjoying the life they've worked so hard to build.

———

Owners of lifestyle businesses—businesses that are set up and run by their founders primarily with the aim of sustaining a particular level of income—often end up with similar regrets even though they've taken a very different approach. Many are happy maintain-ing their businesses without growing them, because they have a "servant" mindset—they meet the needs of others before meeting their own. They are more motivated by bringing value to their cus-tomers than they are by the prospect of creating the next Apple. Unfortunately, without real growth, they are perpetually scram-bling on the hamster wheel of success. They work long hours, just as Ron's client did, and miss out on the personally fulfilling aspects of their life, too. They're afraid of taking a day off, let alone taking a vacation, for fear of losing business.

Some lifestyle business owners wind up with the same problem for a different reason. They spend too much time away from the business pursuing other goals or interests and find that they can't keep pace with the leading firms in their industry. Falling behind their peers jeopardizes the existence of their firms, leaves them financially pinched, and ultimately prevents them from enjoying their life outside of work, too. These business owners end up in the same place, only without the financial security he had to fall back on.

———

To many entrepreneurs, being busy and living a balanced life seem mutually exclusive. You're either working relentlessly with no time for anything else or, if you're enjoying life, you're taking too much time away from the business. We once felt the same way, too—until we achieved the "Sustainable Edge." Today we know it is possible to build a successful business while having plenty of unpressured time to do the things you love. We have proved it in our own firms.

Ron's business, Carson Wealth Management Group, has averaged 27.44 percent growth every year since he started it in 1983 and was recently inducted into the Barron's Hall of Fame[1]. Nonetheless, he has plenty of time for his passions, like spending time with his wife and their children. And although Scott is now growing his firm more quickly than ever, he is transitioning to running it four days a week, so he can spend three days in the dream home he and his wife are building.

We'll show you how you, too, can bring balance to a busy life, without sacrificing growth in your business. No matter how big your goals are for your firm or what challenges the economy throws at you, being busy with balance is a very achievable goal—but only if you make the right decisions that give you the Sustainable Edge.

"By narrowing your focus to just a few passions, you will enjoy your life more than if you try to pursue twenty passions at once."

Creating a Sustainable Edge begins with identifying your major passions so you can build your life around them. First and foremost you must learn how to increase your Business IQ. We'll share our IQ Grower™ process tools in Chapter One to get you started on the

---

1. *Barron's* magazine, October 20, 2014 issue. Advisors inducted into the Hall of Fame include those who were recipients of the Barron's Top 100 Independent Advisors ranking since the list's inception. The Barron's rankings are based on data provided by over 4,000 of the nation's most productive advisors. Factors included in the rankings: assets under management, revenue produced for the firm, regulatory record, quality of practice and philanthropic work. Investment performance isn't an explicit component because not all advisors have audited results and because performance figures often are influenced more by clients' risk tolerance than by an advisor's investment-picking abilities.

right course. Each chapter will build on the IQ Grower™ process and conclude with our IQ Grower™ exercises, designed to take you through the process of helping you create a richer, more rewarding life in just fifteen minutes a week. The more focused you become through the IQ Grower™ exercises, the more effective you will be, and the more willing your team will be to mobilize behind you. That, in turn, will free you to focus on what you're most passionate about at work and in your life. Suddenly, you will be what we call "busy with balance."

Ultimately achieving the Sustainable Edge is not solely about creating a business where you can fulfill your passions. It also means having time for the three or four other things in your life you are passionate about. These might be your family, your faith, good health, French films, bird hunting, or whatever you really care about. By narrowing your focus to just a few passions, you will enjoy your life more than if you try to pursue twenty passions at once. We will help you do that through the ideas and lessons taught in this book.

ACKNOWLEDGMENTS

I truly believe that no one ever creates success on their own. Everyone needs a positive team with supportive people to be with them on their journey. I'm thankful that I've been so blessed with truly amazing people to help me throughout my life.

First, I want to thank my family, especially my wife, Jeanie. You are the glue that holds us all together. Your support over the years has made all the difference, and I would not have a fraction of my success without you. I would not be the man I am today without you. I would also like to thank my children, Chelsie, Madison, and Grant, for reminding me what matters most: True Wealth. I define True Wealth as all that we have that money can't buy and death can't take away. I hope I've been a positive influence on your lives, because you certainly have been to mine. Every day you make me want to be better at what I am to you. My favorite part of the day is asking you guys about your success and living your life by design, not by default. Keep doing what you're passionate about, and thank you for everything you've given me.

I give a HUGE thank you to my parents. They've always been my biggest cheerleaders, supporting and loving me every step of the way. Also, to my sister, who loves me and is always there for me. Her constant ideas, suggestions, encouragement, and feedback are greatly appreciated.

I'd also like to acknowledge my partnership with LPL Financial. My thirty-two-year, and counting, association with them has been amazing. Jim Putnam, Todd Robinson, Robert Moore, Mark Casady, and especially Elyssa Lamoureux, who's not only a great partner today but will also be a great partner in the future.

TD Ameritrade, all the way up from Fred Tomsack, Chairman, Tom Nally, Mike Watson, and all those who have been key partners of ours. You guys do try harder, and it shows.

Edmond Walters, founder of eMoney, you've been a great supporter of mine. We have made a positive difference on our profession, and I thank you for being a part of that with me.

I'd also like to thank all of my CIA partners. You're out there carrying the torch for trust, transparency, and accountability. I'm so proud of what we're doing every day.

And, of course, all the internal stakeholders at the Carson Group of companies—you make work not work, but instead something that's so enjoyable, it's truly one of my passions. For that I thank you. Here's to many more years together.

—**Ron Carson**, Omaha, Nebraska, 2015

I would like to thank God for the gift of family. Thank you to my wife, Angie, who supported this book and everything I do. You have helped me focus on the teachings in this book, such as True Wealth and relationships. To my children, Lakin and Jacob, I am very proud of you. The three of you drive all that I do. I would also like to thank my parents, who have always been there for me.

Many thanks to all the internal stakeholders at Cornerstone Wealth Management, who have helped me learn the power of vulnerability at work—special thanks for your patience in my slow learning curve with this.

I would also like to thank my mentor and friend Ron Carson who has had the biggest impact on the growth and success of Cornerstone Wealth Management.

Many thanks also to Verne Harnish for his works *Scaling Up* and *Mastering the Rockefeller Habits*, which have been instrumental in helping me with priorities, metrics, and meeting rhythms.

I'd also like to thank those we serve. I take your confidence seriously. You drive me every day to make what we do better, so you can focus on True Wealth and relationships.

—**Scott Ford**, Hagerstown, Maryland, 2015

INTRODUCTION:
THE ULTIMATE QUESTION

As owners of our own businesses, we are intimately familiar with the traps that business owners can fall into. Ron founded Carson Wealth Management Group in 1983 and has grown the firm, based in Omaha, into one of the largest wealth advisory firms in the country. Today, Carson Wealth advises on nearly $6 billion in assets. But working around the clock when he started the firm cost him time with his family he can never get back. It is painful for him to admit he missed out on much of the first decade of his oldest daughter's life, because he was dedicating almost all of his time to establishing his firm.

Scott faced his own challenges in juggling a growing business with life outside of work. After founding his fast-growing firm Cornerstone Wealth Management Group in 1996, he grew it tenfold in the first seven years he was in business and, by 2008, was named one of 20 Rising Stars of Wealth Management by *Private Asset Management Magazine*[1]. After years of workaholism, he swung to the other extreme and rarely worked more than a forty-hour week. He had plenty of time to spend with his wife, Angie, and their two children. He also attended church regularly and studied jiu-jitsu in his spare time.

That schedule worked for a while. But like many business owners, Scott struggled to make sense of the new landscape formed by the global financial collapse. As a member of Ron's coaching program, Peak Advisor Alliance, he phoned Ron in Omaha for advice on how to grow his business in 2009.

Ron challenged him to rethink his business with one simple question, "If you don't wake up tomorrow, would your firm be the one you want managing your family's wealth?"

Although Scott's response to Ron's question was, "Yes," he qualified it. "But," he said, "we can always do a better job," even though he knew his firm was the best in his region. In the wake of their tough conversation, he was nagged with doubt. Scott finally realized, after some honest and brutal self-reflection, that his wife and children would be better served if he invested his family's assets with a large national firm, not his lifestyle practice. Cornerstone Wealth just didn't have the budget to capitalize on the new technologies the bigger advisors were using to keep pace with new automated "roboadvisors" and global competition.

---

1. *Institutional Investor News'* "The 20 Rising Stars of Wealth Management" is based on nominations submitted by investment management professionals, selected by publishing staff. Award criteria is based on $1 million dollars in investable assets per private client and demonstrating strong relationship and portfolio skills.

The Sustainable Edge

Since our critical realizations, each of us has made a dramatic turn-around in the way we run our businesses. We have discovered how to run a thriving business while enjoying a meaningful and balanced life built around our passions. We have learned how to create the Sustainable Edge.

When you have the Sustainable Edge, you really can "have it all." This will vary, depending on what your definition of "all" is. For Ron, that means spending time with his wife and children, knowing he's in great health, and knowing that he's having an immeasurable impact on others. Your definition may be very different from ours, but the personal details are not as important as making the right business decisions that will lead to growth. Growth will feed balance in your life. Balance, in turn, will feed more growth. It is a virtuous cycle that will fuel itself in perpetuity. This book will help you define and attain your Sustainable Edge in the complex, fast-changing business world that often seems to conspire against it.

So what exactly does it mean to have it all? It means having a life that is full of the relationships and rewards—personal, emotional, and spiritual—that really matter to you. It is having the freedom to enjoy experiences you will always treasure with the people who matter most in your life and the lifetime memories that result and sustain you. It means having the ability and emotional wherewithal to do things for others without expecting anything in return. It is about savoring each day you are blessed to live and spending it as you would if you knew it were your last.

By definition, having it all is unique to each of us. For Ron, having it all means he has been able to grow the business he loves while having time to take one-on-one trips with each of his three children to pursue the activities they enjoy, from camping to attending the Sundance Film Festival. One reminder of how "rich" Ron has really become came as he prepared to give a toast at his daughter's recent wedding. Having freed plenty of time to spend with her while she was growing up, his biggest challenge was cutting back on the memories he would share so he would not bore his guests. Ron has it "all" in his professional relationships as well. He savored a moment at a recent conference when business owners told him how he had improved their lives in immeasurable ways. Scott and Ron shared another "have it all" moment during a recent hunting retreat where they were able to bask in a spectacular, sunny day and enjoy a deep conversation.

For Scott, having it all has meant different things, like the freedom to share breakfast with his father, who recently passed, every Friday for the last three years of his life. Scott takes comfort in the fact that he didn't leave anything he wanted to say to his dad unsaid. To him, that knowledge is worth more than any amount of money. Having it all means pursuing a dream he and his wife, Angie, have shared to build a rustic home in the wilderness surrounded by edible landscaping, where they will live off the land, now that their children are grown.

Achieving the joys of having it all takes planning. You must first figure out what it means to you and then build your priorities around it. In the following chapters, we'll show you how to tap into your subconscious, using the IQ Grower™ process, to uncover your deepest dreams. Then we'll help you close the "knowing-doing gap" that keeps so many entrepreneurs from achieving their dreams. Having it all is not about adding things to your to-do list. It's about stripping them away, so you have more time to enjoy life's richness. Still, achieving it requires commitment. You must commit to growing your business by a minimum of 15 percent or more each year to attain and maintain it. That pace of growth creates the breathing room you need to achieve balance, which, in turn, will lead to more growth.

"You must commit to grow your business by a minimum of 15 percent each year to have it all."

The 15 Percent Growth Imperative

Once you achieve at least 15 percent growth annually in your firm, you will find that it is easier to be busy with balance. Then, as you become more focused through the IQ Grower™ exercises, you will become more effective, and your team will become more willing to mobilize behind you. That synergy in your team, in turn, will free you to focus on what you're most passionate about at your company and in your life. Suddenly, you will be what we call busy with balance. Fifteen percent annual growth seems to be the magic number that will give you the peace of mind and financial freedom to enjoy the deepest passions in your life. In turn, you will be freed to nurture the other aspects of your life that gave you the perspective you needed to reach greater heights in your business. You don't have to sacrifice growth to achieve balance. By realizing this, you are well on your way to achieving the Sustainable Edge.

———

Ron's coaching program, Peak Advisor Alliance, currently works with advisors in more than 1,100 firms around the country. He has found that when businesses grow at a rate slower than 15 percent annually, they are not sustainable. Firms with very slow or flat growth just don't have the ability, confidence, energy, or vibe to prosper. When you grow at least 15 percent—ideally 18 to 20 percent—you will have the capital you need to invest in remaining robust and healthy. As your firm expands, you will be able to offer the growth path, culture, and energy that will attract the top talent you need to be competitive.

"Sustaining at least 15 percent annual growth will give you the mental space to step out of the fray, consider your options carefully, and make decisions from a position of strength."

This is especially true now, with steamroller forces like automation and globalization bearing down on many firms. Digital technology has brought new efficiencies but also dangerous lures and complexity that can devour your time and throw your businesses off track. "Never have the opportunities to succeed been greater, nor have the distractions that can cause you to fail," as Ron put it in a speech at an Excel meeting with 500 business owners in 2009 in Scottsdale, Arizona. Sustaining at least 15 percent annual growth will give you the mental space to step out of the fray, consider your options carefully, and make decisions from a position of strength. If you're growing your business more slowly than 15 percent, you'll be too busy scrambling for your next customer to do anything else.

How you define 15 percent growth depends on the critical benchmarks in your industry. In many firms, the crucial growth you need is in revenue or profits. In a wealth management firm, it is in assets under management. Measure growth as you would measure oxygen in a body—growth is the critical element for a business to survive.

Of course, it is difficult to achieve 15 percent growth if you don't have a clear mission or a vision for achieving that growth. We will show you how to tap into your subconscious to figure out your "Why"—the reason your firm exists in the first place—so that you can set the goals that will help you pursue what matters to you and use your goals to shape your daily priorities.

But what if your dream is running a small boutique firm? Can you grow it at a more measured pace? We will not try to convince you to build a giant firm, if that is not your goal. We both know many entrepreneurs who prefer the lifestyle of running a smaller business. However, if you are happy maintaining your business without growing it, we can show you how changing your mindset will give you more time and more energy to pursue your passions in life.

Settling for little or no growth or is no longer a viable long-term option in today's marketplace. Depending on your industry, it may not even be a reasonable short-term option. If your business is not growing by at least 15 percent a year, you are not keeping pace with the ongoing and rapid change in your industry. Remember the question Ron posed to Scott—the ultimate question, "If you don't wake up tomorrow, would your firm be the one you want managing your family's wealth?" In this book we will show you exactly why hitting a minimum of 15 percent annual growth will allow you to answer "Yes" and will give you the freedom to have it all. We'll also show you how to expand your business at that steady pace.

We won't ask you to shoehorn time-consuming new tasks into your schedule. Instead, we want to set you up to be busy with balance. We will ask you to pare back the distractions that are draining your time and energy, so that you have more freedom to enjoy what really matters. The positive changes you make in your business will perpetuate themselves once you put them in place, without long-term extra effort on your part.

Our ideas are not theories. We have tested them on the front lines of our own businesses every day. We are confident you will come away with many ideas you can immediately put to use to create a better business and a richer life for you and the people who matter most to you.

We encourage every business owner to make a critical decision today. Will you let your business crowd out everything else you value in life? If you're ready to have it all in your business and your life, we are ready to show you the way.

THE IQ GROWER™ PROCESS: 15 MINUTES A WEEK TO A HIGHER BUSINESS IQ

Ron often speaks to entrepreneurs who cannot understand why their firms are not growing faster. Often, he'll begin by posing a question, "Who in this room has a high IQ?" He is almost always met with silence.

He'll scan the room and catch a business owner's eye. "So what's your IQ?" he'll ask directly.

More silence. "Well . . . ," the business owner might finally say. "I know it's high."

In reality, Ron doesn't care about the Intelligence Quotient. So he'll ask, "How many of you in this room feel that 'when all is said and done, much more gets said than gets done?'"

Invariably, every hand in the room will shoot up. Unbeknownst to them, they have just answered Ron's original question. As smart as these business owners are, and no matter how high their Intelligence Quotient may be, they almost always have a low implementation quotient of making their goals into reality. In fact, some of them cannot even articulate their goals, be they short- or long-term, personal or professional. Knowing your goals and making them a reality—that's the "IQ" Ron cares about.

Do you have a low implementation quotient? Most business owners realize they do when Ron shares this story. While they are busier than ever, they aren't nailing their goals, nor are they anywhere near achieving the minimum 15 percent growth, essential to winning the Sustainable Edge. They often have no real endgame or succession plan in mind. This lack of focus or clarity can lead to crises at work that, in turn, cause an unbalanced personal life. An unbalanced personal life can lead to poor decisions at work, which can end up perpetuating a vicious cycle.

Some owners have a high implementation quotient at the office but not in their personal life. They aren't clear on what really matters to them at the end of the workday. They are highly productive at work but fail to set or achieve important goals outside of work, like sustaining a happy marriage, sharing a close relationship with their children, or simply taking the necessary time to recharge their batteries.

Blueprinting your life through the IQ Grower™ process is one way to become proactive and really figure out what you want for yourself and your life. The IQ Grower™ process will help you to live in the moment, so you really enjoy the miracle of life. So often people miss out on the moment because, like the unhappy business owner Ron met, they are caught up in doing what they think society wants them to do and not what really matters to them.

The IQ Grower™ process will free you to live your life by design and not by default, so that you will not end up like the client mentioned in the Preface. Raising your implementation quotient can save you from falling into the rut most Americans are in: They are on an unconscious journey to arrive safely at death. It is so easy to fall into a routine where your days, weeks, and months pass you by so that when you reach the end of your life, you find yourself saying, "I wish I had . . ." We want everyone we meet to be able to say "I'm glad I did . . . ," not "I wish I had . . ."

What Steve Jobs Knew

If you don't set goals and priorities for yourself, life will live you, not the other way around. No one put this better than Steve Jobs in his commencement speech at Stanford in 2005, soon after he was diagnosed with pancreatic cancer. "Your time is limited, so don't waste it living someone else's life. Don't be trapped by dogma. . . . Don't let the noise of others' opinions drown out your own inner voice. And most important, have the courage to follow your heart and intuition. . . . Everything else is secondary."

We want you to lead a Steve Jobs life—but on your own terms.

That's why we created the IQ Grower™ process. By using the process, you will learn what is most important to achieving your dream—not what society thinks it should be. You'll learn to identify the passions that are most important to you and the goals that matter most. You'll be able to achieve what matters to you most—in the key areas of your life. The IQ Grower™ exercises may seem simple but they are the seminal step to achieving the Sustainable Edge. Don't underestimate their extraordinary power to change your life.

From Blueprinting to Raising your Implementation Quotient

In Ron's previous books, *Avalanche* and *Tested in the Trenches*, and through his coaching program, Peak Advisor Alliance, he has shared his Blueprinting process, a system that helps wealth advisors and other business owners achieve the Sustainable Edge. Blueprinting is a process that allows you to live life by design, not by default. It provides a roadmap to guide you—from start to finish—to find meaning and purpose in life. This process has helped countless wealth advisors and business owners achieve the Sustainable Edge. While Ron is living proof that Blueprinting works, he has found that many business owners don't stick with it. In fact, Scott has grappled with completing the challenge himself and had to return to the process three times to complete it. The first time he tried it, in 2001, he rushed through and didn't dig deeply enough to be really honest about what was important to him.

Scott's experience isn't surprising. Blueprinting has tremendous power and can unleash an immense amount of focus and energy that very few people will experience in their life. But it can be scary at first ("What will I find out about myself?"). It requires being truthful about what you really want out of the rest of your life and a willingness to push beyond easy answers, like claiming work is your only passion. Although you may be a little fearful of digging deeply, once you do, you'll be amazed at what you discover.

Frustrated by watching business owners miss out on the rewards of Blueprinting, Ron and Scott developed the IQ Grower™ process, an abbreviated version of the Blueprinting technique that requires just fifteen minutes a week. In those powerful fifteen minutes, you will begin to achieve life-changing results. We are certain that experiencing the rewards will inspire you to complete the full Blueprinting process, which is included in the appendix of this book, and progress even further in your journey within another six months to a year. When you set goals in the IQ Grower™ process, you may dramatically overestimate what you can accomplish in the short-term. But, if you stick with it you will dramatically underestimate what you can achieve in the next decade. One of Ron's favorite quotes is, "The past is bedrock unchangeable. Forget about it. The future is clay to be molded day by day." Blueprinting supplies the clay so that you can remake each day.

> *"Committing to the IQ Grower™ process will give you the courage to pursue what really matters to you while you have the time to act on it."*

We urge you to express how you honestly feel when you dive into the IQ Grower™ exercises. Most people cannot immediately confront their true feelings. They will put on paper goals or ideas that are contrary to what they know to be true. But it feels amazing to be truthful and true to yourself. Remember, you don't have to share the exercises with anyone else. Put them in your safe deposit box if you must. The beauty of the IQ Grower™ process is that you don't have to be facing a terminal illness like Steve Jobs to achieve his perspective. The IQ Grower™ exercises will help you tap into wisdom that most people never experience until on their deathbeds.

Ultimately, by tapping into this wisdom, you can make great strides in striking an effective work-life balance. The exercises will give you the courage to pursue what really matters to you while you still have the time to act on it. By being truly honest with yourself, you will get to a place where you don't care how people judge you, and you will be able to harness the passions you never dared to set loose before.

IDENTIFY WHAT YOU VALUE MOST

If you are clear on what is important to you in life, it will be infinitely easier to set the right priorities. To do so, list at least six things you value most in life and rank them in order of importance. Next to each one, indicate the actual percentage of your time you spend living and supporting these values. Examples of things you might list include family, work, community, spiritual fulfillment, generosity, and adventure.

	Most important values	Percentage of time spent living and supporting my values
1.		
2.		
3.		
4.		
5.		
6.		

You may discover that you are spending your time on something that no longer matters to you. One wealth manager Ron knows realized her true passion was outside of her practice, so she sold it. She now runs a nonprofit in a developing country.

IDENTIFY THE PERSONALLY MEANINGFUL ACTIVITIES TO WHICH YOU ARE COMMITTED

Many business owners overbook their calendars with activities they don't enjoy and that will mean little to them when they look back on their lives. By pinpointing the activities on which you truly want to spend your time, it will be easier to say "yes" to them and "no" to the activities that drain you.

If you are not sure what you really want to do with your time, answer the following questions that may help you identify the most meaningful activities for you.

1. What are your unique gifts? _____

   _____

   _____

2. What do you do extremely well? _____

   _____

   _____

3. What activities give you a great feeling of satisfaction and fulfillment? _____

   _____

   _____

4. What social issues are you so passionate about you would write an editorial about them in your local newspaper or post a comment online advocating your position? _____

   _____

   _____

5. Given a choice, do you prefer to help people by rolling up your sleeves and pitching in, or do you prefer a more

behind-the-scenes role? Give examples of the types of activities you like to do based on your response. _____

_____

_____

6. When you feel empty and directionless in life, what is missing in your life during those times that is causing you to feel that way? _____

_____

_____

7. How are you nourishing your soul spiritually? _____

_____

_____

8. If you live your life with meaningful purpose, how will the world be a better place? _____

_____

_____

9. How will you know you are living your life with meaningful purpose? _____

_____

10. If you received $1 billion what would you be doing and how would you use that money? _____

_____

_____

Some people who complete the list find that their favorite activities don't fit into the lifestyle their spouses or families want. If you truly desire to build a life around your passions, and your spouse or other important person is not supportive, we encourage you to give some thought to how you will reconcile those differences. Finances are another issue to consider, of course, especially if you have recently invested heavily in your business. Do you view a lack of money as an impediment to fully realizing your meaningful purpose? If so, what are some creative ways that you can address and overcome this issue?

It may be tempting to pick activities that you think make you look good to others even though they are not what you truly enjoy. Remember, the tough question Ron asked Scott? We recommend speaking with a close confidante who can keep you honest with yourself. The idea of this exercise is to free you from meaningless perceived and/or real obligations, so that you can have more time and energy to pursue the activities about which you are most passionate.

DEFINE YOUR ESSENTIAL SIX AND YOUR MOST VITAL GOALS

If there is nothing else you take away from this book, the "Essential Six" and "Most Vital" exercise is the most important. It will transform your life as soon as you begin to use it and probably even before you finish. In the Essential Six you will identify your top six professional priorities for each day; the Most Vital is the big goal you must accomplish for the week.

Before you leave the office at the end of each day, list the Essential Six important things you must accomplish the following day, in order of importance, and add them to your calendar. Doing this the night before allows your subconscious to begin to work on your tasks in advance—to prepare for the day ahead. Begin your day by tackling item number one on your list. Do not move on to number two until you have successfully completed the first task. Tony Schwartz, author of *Be Excellent at Anything*, has found that working in ninety-minute increments, followed by short breaks, is the best way to maximize your productivity. We have found his suggestion to be helpful and a good rule of thumb for completing your Essential Six.

For Scott, the Most Vital for the week is almost always tied to the number one company priority for the quarter. If not, it is tied to one of his personal key performance indicators (KPIs) for the quarter. The first on the list of Essential Six is typically tied to the Most Vital for the week. Scott tries to dedicate the first ninety minutes of his day to working on it alone, usually before anyone else is in the office. The remaining five are usually a little more task oriented but still what he considers a great use of his time—like working out, meeting with a valued prospect or client, making a potential tuck-in or acquisition call, attending a webinar, or going on a date with his wife.

Don't worry or stress if you are not able to get through all six items every day. If you are able to accomplish all six priorities every day, you may be setting the bar too low for yourself. Reevaluate the tasks on your Essential Six. By focusing on your most important priority every day and crossing it off your list first, you will be surprised by how much more you accomplish overall.

Sometimes, your schedule will get derailed before you have completed every item on the list. Perhaps a major client will ask for an unexpected meeting or an urgent situation arises at home. The IQ Grower™ process is designed with that in mind. You will be surprised by how your awareness of the list will help you return to it and complete it, even if it is later in the day than you thought. For instance, not long ago a pipe burst at Scott's home, and he had to deal with the flood immediately. After taking care of the flood, he still had two important but incomplete items on his Essential Six list. When he returned to his desk late in the evening, he easily finished them. Without his Essential Six list—and the power of his subconscious mind that had been ruminating on the tasks on his list all day—those items probably would have fallen by the wayside in the wake of the burst pipe.

To make sure you are focusing on the right priorities, evaluate each item on your Essential Six list each day and ask yourself if you are really pursuing what you are good at and enjoy. Otherwise, you must overhaul your list until you can answer "yes."

It is also essential that you set your Most Vital for the week—the top goal you truly must accomplish. Naming it at the end of the week—perhaps on a Friday evening before going home, or over the weekend—gives your subconscious the opportunity to work on it, so you will have clarity of vision as you begin your next week. For example, one of Scott's most recent vital goals is to build the timeline and steps to implement his acquisition and tuck-in plan for Cornerstone Wealth in 2015. When you set your intention on what you really want to achieve, it will become much easier to say no to distractions. You'll find yourself delegating or avoiding unnecessary phone calls, emails, and meetings that distract you from the important work of the day and keep you working late into the evening.

As creative people, entrepreneurs rarely meet an idea they don't love. We suffer from overconfidence and like to believe we can be good at everything. But as our initial enthusiasm fades, we quickly abandon these initiatives and move on to the next. The more focused you become through the Essential Six and Most Vital exercise, the more effective you will be, and the more willing your team will be to mobilize behind your latest initiative. That, in turn, will free you to focus on what you're most passionate about at your company. Suddenly, you will be busy with balance.

Once you are crystal clear on what truly matters to you, it will become easier to decide on your most important goals for next quarter and ten to twenty-five years from now. Base your goals on what you value most. Many people set their goals in areas such as attitude, career, education, family, health, finance, recreation, community, or spiritual life. Use these suggestions to get you started visualizing your own areas of improvement or goals. The goals you choose should truly reflect what matters most to you. When you have completed your list, we recommend you laminate it and keep it with you. That will keep them top of mind. (Ron hangs his in the shower!)

Once you have identified your short- and long-term goals, ask yourself the following questions:

- Do your company and work reflect your personal values?

- Do your company and work give your life purpose?

- Do your company and work provide the resources to enable you to achieve your personal goals?

- What are your goals for being in business?

- What is your endgame?

TAP INTO YOUR SUBCONSCIOUS

Preparing for a conference call with his coaches, Ron reviewed a Blueprinting exercise he had completed on that same date twenty years prior. He was surprised to discover that he had accomplished everything he wanted to do in the intervening twenty years. But when he looked back at his one-year goal for that same year, he had only accomplished 52 percent of it. We can't tell you why the process works this way, but it often does. The IQ Grower™ exercises—based on the same Blueprinting process Ron had used—work the same way.

We tend to dramatically underestimate what we can get done over a ten- to twenty-year time frame and drastically overestimate what we can get done in the next three to twelve months. Keep that in mind while going through this process. With that said, however, the IQ Grower™ process will help you jumpstart your short-term goals, even if you do overestimate what you can get done in the near term. For example, during a difficult period for his family in 2012, Scott listed family harmony as one of his goals. Today his family has achieved that harmony beyond any of his expectations. The same held true in 2013 when he listed a goal he shared with his wife, Angie, buying a log home in the woods where they could live the pared-down life they both desired. They found the home they dreamed of and soon after closed the deal to buy it. Consciously committing to a goal that stems from your deepest desires will help you start moving toward it in ways that may never be completely clear to you, because you are tapping into your subconscious and channeling your "Why."

APPRECIATE THE NOW

Setting goals is essential to your success, but it is equally important to savor and appreciate the present. Looking back on your past and the progress you have made toward achieving the Sustainable Edge will help keep you happy and fulfilled.

We recommend that you keep a gratitude journal and record what you are grateful for each day, whether it is the beautiful scenery you can see from the window of your office or an act of kindness you received or gave. It doesn't matter if you write for five minutes or an hour—the act of putting to paper the experiences or actions for which you're grateful will make a positive impact on your day. Your life will become much more joyful when you make a conscious effort to notice and enjoy your daily experiences, from a trip down a familiar road to an especially good cup of coffee. At the core of achieving the Sustainable Edge is taking the time to replenish yourself—acknowledging and celebrating the joys in your life is an essential part of that.

MAKE IT HAPPEN

You can make it happen and achieve the Sustainable Edge in your business and life. And it starts with devoting just fifteen minutes a week to the IQ Grower™ process. If you devote the time each week, you will achieve amazing results. A good way to begin is by blocking off fifteen minutes on your calendar each week for the next quarter to make time to work on the exercises.

Ideally, you should work on the exercises at the same time every week in order for it to become part of your regular rhythm. Do each exercise as honestly as you can in the time you've allotted. Perfection is not important. You can always return to the exercises later.

Most entrepreneurs are action-takers. Our bias is toward doing, not "paralysis by analysis." That orientation is vital to growing a business, but it can prevent you from getting in touch with what really matters to you. So we know that the kind of self-reflection we're calling for here might not be up your alley. But it's an important exercise, and it will help you counteract that tendency.

IQ Grower™ Exercises

Identify what you value most.

List at least six things you value most in life and rank them in order of importance. Next to each one, indicate the actual percentage of your time you spend living and supporting these values.

1. _____

2. _____

3. _____

4. _____

5. _____

6. _____

Do you recognize the feeling of being busy without balance?

Can you identify what is occupying too much of your time?

Has it affected your personal effectiveness in the office or at home?

Do you ever feel like you are living a life that you didn't plan for yourself or that your work is running your life?

What is your "Passion that Pays"? Visualize what it might look like to implement it.

Make time for the IQ Grower™ process.

Block off fifteen minutes on your calendar each week for the next quarter.

For best results, work on the exercises at the same time each week.

Resource Link

Managing Your Energy for Productivity

http://www.actionablebooks.com/en-ca/summaries/be
-excellent-at-anything/

IQ Grower™ Process: Daily

Do this before leaving the office or before going to bed.

---

1 **WHAT IS MY ATTITUDE OF GRATITUDE?**

List 3 things you are grateful for today and 3 things you hope to be grateful for tomorrow.

Today	Tomorrow
1.	1.
2.	2.
3.	3.

---

2 **WHAT ACTIVITIES DRIVE MY QUARTERLY GOALS/PRIORITIES?**

List your number 1 thing to accomplish for tomorrow,
then list the 6 most important thin to accomplish tomorrow in priority order.

Vital 1	How Good (HG) 1–10	How Excited (HE) 1–10

6 Most		
Goals	(HG) 1–10	(HE) 1–10

IQ Grower™ Process: Quarterly

Do this every 3 months.
What you value may not change, but priorities and goals for the quarter will.

---

1 **WHAT I VALUE MOST & WHAT IS THE MOST MEANINGFUL TO ME?**
List in order of priority the things you value most and are most meaningful to you.

1. _____   4. _____

2. _____   5. _____

3. _____   6. _____

---

2 **BHAG "BIG HAIRY AUDACIOUS GOAL" FROM JIM COLLINS**
List your 6 most important goals for 10-25 years from now.

1. _____   4. _____

2. _____   5. _____

3. _____   6. _____

---

3 **WHAT ARE MY GOALS FOR THIS QUARTER**
THAT WILL MOVE ME IN THE DIRECTION OF MY BHAG?
When you are finished, pick the most important of the 6 goals to focus on for the quarter and circle it.

1. _____   4. _____

2. _____   5. _____

3. _____   6. _____

2.

HARNESS YOUR SUBCONSCIOUS TO IDENTIFY YOUR WHY

Not long ago, Robert Moore, former president of LPL Financial and current CEO of Legal & General Investment Management America, had a candid conversation with Ron about the competitive dynamics in the financial services industry. Since the Great Recession, the "performance bar has to be continually raised in order to deliver sustainable results and industry leadership," Moore was clear in stating. Moore continues, "We cannot afford the luxury of not finishing the last thing before moving on." For LPL Financial, this translates into a complete focus on the fundamentals of its business.

By saying no to many potentially lucrative opportunities, LPL Financial is growing rapidly while thoughtfully managing its growth. Its leadership team is completely committed to the company's Why—its singular focus on enabling independent business owners to deliver objective advice. This clarity of purpose allows the company to grow and thrive without constantly chasing the next shiny object.

If you want your business or practice to thrive, you must be crystal clear on your own Why. In some companies, this is easy. The Why is obvious. But in many firms, it is harder to uncover. There may be several potential Whys. Your work as a leader is to determine your company's Why and make sure your team is aligned around it. Knowing your Why will help you make the right choices.

The most important Why lies deep in your subconscious. As Napoleon Hill pointed out in his classic book *Think and Grow Rich*, for every bit of information in your conscious mind, there are billions of bits in your subconscious mind. Being able to source the information in your subconscious mind when you need it is the key to operating in the "zone." Having a strong Why allows you to feed and maintain a Sustainable Edge.

When you hit a perfect golf shot automatically, it is because you have tapped instantly into your subconscious mind. The same holds true in your business. When the idea for a great new product comes to you suddenly while you are hiking, or the perfect phrase pops into your mind as you are giving a speech, it is because you are tapping into your subconscious. Your subconscious is like a Google bot—it's hard at work in the background and, ideally, surfacing information when you most need it. When you are not actively concentrating, your best insights will arrive. That channeling of your subconscious mind will give you the Sustainable Edge.

Take time to write down your answers to the IQ Grower™ exercises, but expect unexpected moments of clarity. When Scott was working on his last book, *Financial Jiu-Jitsu*, he struggled to weave his ideas into a whole and simplify them. He worked at it for six months, during which time he attended a conference in Hawaii with his wife. The beach isn't Scott's idea of a good time, but as he sat under the umbrella with Angie, reading and thinking, the whole message of the book appeared to him with extreme clarity. Taking advantage of "think time" and allowing his subconscious to work allowed that moment of clarity to come.

Ron's biggest revelations have come when he was energized by doing yoga, biking, or other activities where he allows his subconscious to communicate with his conscious mind. He notices he has the greatest clarity when he spends time by himself in nature meditating, thinking, and appreciating life. These types of activities tend to provide him with more insights than months of working at his daily routine.

Your subconscious can also warn you of dangers that can hurt your business. Recently, another advisory firm approached Ron about sponsoring an event. He had met the firm's principals several times, but he did not feel comfortable forming a relationship with them. Call it a gut feeling or an instinct—something in their interactions triggered Ron's subconscious to warn him against moving forward with the sponsorship. The deal could have earned a lot of money for his firm, but he politely declined, explaining that his firm already had enough sponsors for their event. Not long after that conversation, this advisory firm encountered a series of troubles that showed Ron he had made the right decision. He's glad he trusted his subconscious, and because he regularly took time to tap into his subconscious he was able to heed the warning he received when faced with an important decision.

So how do you plunge into your subconscious mind and discover your Why? One of the best ways we know is to use our IQ Grower™. This process will help you arrive at your Essential Six and Most Vital, so you can reach your key goals and transcend the uncertainty and market shifts that might otherwise threaten your success.

If you can commit fifteen minutes a week to the IQ Grower™ process, you will be surprised at how quickly you can raise your Why to the surface of everything you do. The insights you gain through the IQ Grower™ process and by using the Essential Six and Most Vital exercise will help you focus and accomplish the things that are really important to you.

Achieve Your Biggest Goals: How to Stay Focused on Your Why

When you are clear on your big goals, it gets easier to say the three magic words that will present you from veering off course, "No, thank you." If you are successful in your business, you will receive many invitations to join boards, meet someone for drinks, or help a good cause. IQ Grower™ will help you protect your time and say no to activities that don't move the needle on what matters most to you. If you cannot see clearly from the beginning where requests and demands on your time will lead or how they are tied into your Essential Six and Most Vital, it serves you best to say no to them. Committing to activities that flow from your subconscious is the key to being busy with balance and keeping the Sustainable Edge.

Ron made an important statement at Carson Wealth's most recent annual retreat. The retreats are designed to get everyone together to workshop and set the company's most important goals for the coming year. When the group finalized the exercise, Ron held up a sign above the list of goals that read, "No new." He was making the bold statement that he did not want Carson Wealth to experience another year of "commitment creep," where the list would grow throughout the year to include more and more goals. Whenever internal stakeholders attempted to add a goal to the list, he held up the sign, effectively acting as a goalie to block anything else from coming into the net. You might be wondering, "Why not try to get more done? If someone has a good idea, why not implement it?" Ron knows from personal experience that trying to add too many goals to the list puts the firm at risk of accomplishing none of them. He was once the worst offender on this front. Now his message is simple: Commit and Complete. In this case, less is truly more.

———

Testing the waters before committing to a new project will help keep you on track. Before Ron commits to a new initiative, like Carson Institutional Alliance, his cutting-edge solution for elite business owners and advisors who are committed to being consumer advocates. His motto is start small, think big, scale fast. If the experiments pay off, then Carson Wealth gets aggressive in its implementation. Constantly creating new targets takes teams off course and distracts them from what has been decided to be mission critical. Chasing new and untested goals forces teams to run in circles, instead of intentionally focusing on accomplishing meaningful results.

Staying focused on your Why requires discipline and personal processes to help you maintain that discipline. When someone introduces a new idea at a quarterly meeting of Scott's firm, Cornerstone Wealth, he requires his team to discuss and vet it thoroughly before he commits any resources. Giving ideas time to percolate is important. This practice prevents you from getting sucked into the enthusiasm for novel and exciting, though not necessarily important, activities. For instance, buying the building where your office is located may seem like a great investment. However, if you are a wealth advisor, you may discover that having to act as landlord or superintendent takes time away from your more important work of investing. Do you really have time in your day to run your firm and be the person whom the roofer calls to discuss a leak, or the person with whom the gardener wants to discuss landscaping? No matter what profit you will earn from owning the building, it may not be worth it if it takes you away from leading your company.

Being disciplined in your goals is especially difficult when it comes to accepting new business that could distract you from your focus or that may not be a good fit with your culture and goals. When a client wants to spend money with your firm, it is very tempting to say yes.

An advisor on Ron's team once asked if he should bring on a client who had complained bitterly that his last advisors did not know what they were doing. Ron sensed that this client would be impossible to satisfy and that the day would come when the client would say the same things about his firm. He sensed that Carson Wealth might regret taking on the new client, but he left the decision to the advisor. Noting that he shared common personal interests with the potential client, the advisor decided to give the new relationship a chance. Both the advisor and the potential client had attended the same college and often ran into each other at basketball games. As Ron had suspected, the honeymoon didn't last long. The client quickly became demanding and rude. Eventually, the advisor came back to Ron asking for tips on how to fire the client. Dealing with the situation became a big distraction from other important business the advisor could have been pursuing.

Committing to the IQ Grower™ process can help you spot clients or activities that are not a good fit for the culture of your firm or its goals. We have all found ourselves in situations where, because of an unexpected distraction—a personal illness, the death of a loved one, a business setback—we lose focus on our key goals. It's easy in these situations to lose sight of how your goals fit in to your current situation. Most people become so mired in managing the distraction that they abandon their goals altogether and never return to them. Looking back at your IQ Grower™ exercises and beginning the process again will help you regain critical focus. It will remind you where you left off so that you can pick right back up, even if you are in a funk. Reviewing the intentions you set out in the IQ Grower™ exercises will give you the strength to act, even when your motivation is lacking.

We assure you, the rewards are immense. Nothing underscored this more for Ron than giving his father-of-the-bride speech at his daughter's wedding. He'd prepared all of his remarks well in advance and, until about an hour before the speech, felt very calm. But as the moment approached, he became overwhelmed with emotion as he thought of toasting to his baby girl's new life. Ron's speech was so heartfelt and rich with memories, that many of his normally buttoned-up entrepreneurs shared that they had been moved to tears as they heard about the many moments of joy Ron and his daughter had experienced together. He never would have had those special memories had he not broken the cycle of workaholism and achieved the Sustainable Edge.

IQ Grower™ Exercises to Harness Your Subconscious

What is your company's Why? _____

_____

_____

As a leader, have you truly considered your personal Why? If so, what is it? _____

_____

_____

Are there places or settings where you can relax and allow your subconscious to work? If so, list them here. If you don't have any places yet, this is a great opportunity to create a list of some different places to try out to see which work best for you.

_____

_____

What daily activities would help you be more in touch with your subconscious? Hint: If you're having trouble getting started, choosing things that help you relax and clear your mind will be helpful. Some examples include meditation, exercise, yoga, and journaling. _____

_____

_____

Can you remember an occasion where your subconscious revealed the solution to a problem or really provided clarity in a situation? If so, what was it? _____

_____

_____

Are you concerned about "commitment creep?" List all your current commitments in order of their priority to you. Can any be removed from your list? Be on the lookout for any that do not contribute to your Essential Six or Most Vital. _____

_____

_____

Are you considering, or have you ever, said no to a request for your time or participation in a new project? Why or why not? If you can cite an example, can you tap into the clarity or strength that allowed you to say no? _____

_____

_____

Resource Link

Identify Your Why:

www.startwithwhy.com

3.

IDENTIFY YOUR PASSION THAT PAYS

What are you deeply passionate about? At what can you be the very best in the world? What drives your business's economic engine?

Many people know what their passions are, but that's as far as they go. They have many passions, are generalists about all of them, and don't strongly commit to one or two. As a result, they never become really exceptional at anything—and this holds true for their businesses, as well. To really find your niche in life, we encourage you to explore and dig deeper into your passions. In doing so, you will reach another level of richness in your business and your life.

Viewing your work as your "Passion that Pays" is the heart of being busy with balance. If your business is truly a passion, it will be much easier to achieve balance in the rest of your life. Work will energize you, so you're ready to enjoy your other passions. Partaking in your other passions will, in turn, put you in the relaxed frame of mind that makes it easier for you to grow your business. Once you pinpoint what your passions are, you can to transform the way you manage your time, so you are spending most of it on what you truly love. That will make it easier to clear your calendar of time-consuming obligations that drain the life out of you.

"Once you give yourself the space to focus on what is most meaningful and fun for you at work, you can tap into the mindset that unlocks new opportunities for you."

What if you're not feeling particularly passionate about your business right now? The IQ Grower™ process will help you figure out the Why behind this, so you can change things to create the necessary shift. But for now let's talk about some of the reasons that connection between passion and profit gets broken. Many entrepreneurs lose their passion, because they try to handle too many tasks in their business on their own. It burns them out. In our experience they often become much more passionate about their business if they focus on the parts they are best suited to handle and surround themselves with bright, capable people to tackle the rest. Once they give themselves the space to focus on what is most meaningful and fun for them at work, they tap into a mindset that unlocks new opportunities. We have found this to be true in our own businesses.

One aspect of running Carson Wealth that Ron particularly enjoys is sharing his personal passions—from hunting to aviation to fine wines—with clients. Not only does Ron have a passion that pays, he also doesn't distinguish between work and play. To him, it's all living. He is doing what he loves to do all the time. Recently Ron was in Napa Valley meeting with a valued client to build on their relationship. He asked the client to introduce him to two other prospects who shared their love of wine as they met at a winery and sipped an amazing vintage. What part of that was work and what part was play? The point is there is no distinction. It was all Ron's passion. Immerse yourself in what you love, and you'll never have to "work" another day.

The more you focus on clients who can share the passions you enjoy, the more fun you will have at work and the easier it will be to grow your business. Recently, another valued client of Ron's bought a new plane and flew to Omaha to show it to him. The client arrived with a prospect who shared their mutual passion for aviation and bird hunting. Ron had encouraged him to make introductions to people with their same passions—an easy thing for the client to do. All three of them ended up heading to Ron's hunting lodge, where Ron got to know the new prospect while doing something they all enjoyed. As Plato said, "You can discover more about a person in an hour of play than in a year of conversation."

> *"You can discover more about a person in an hour of play than in a year of conversation."*

At another recent meeting, Ron met a major client at a winery to discuss business. When the owner of the winery asked how they knew each other, Ron's client said, "He's been our family's wealth manager for twenty years." Not long after Ron returned to his office, he received an email from the winery's owner. The owner asked if he could discuss his own family's finances with Ron. Keep in mind, even if your business is at an earlier stage of growth than Ron's is, running it does not have to be a grueling slog. Tapping into your passions is still the best route to growth.

Look back at your youth and you'll often find your deepest passions started there. That's certainly true for Scott. Ever since he ran his first business as a teenage magician, entertaining children at birthday parties, he has had a lifelong passion for reading and learning about entrepreneurship. When he was thrust into situations where he couldn't act on that passion, his enthusiasm waned. For instance, when he was in high school, he had to write a term paper in his junior year. When the day came to turn it in, he didn't have a paper to submit. He had no interest in reading a book and writing about it. His teacher was flabbergasted. "In my twenty-six years of teaching, I have never had a student not turn in a term paper," she said. He still can't believe he passed the class. During his senior year, however, he was required to take an oral exam for which he was free to pick the topic. Scott decided to speak about motivation and goals, a subject that always intrigued him. He read Denis Waitley and several other writers on the topic and received an A-plus on his presentation.

When Scott looks back, it's clear he has always been an entrepreneur. It is in his DNA. If he weren't in wealth management, he would be an entrepreneur doing something else. Meanwhile, he has to chuckle at the irony of the fact that he is writing his third book. Now that he is writing on topics he is really into, the process is fun. It's not work. He can only imagine how his junior-year English teacher would react if he sent the books to her. In running his firm, he frequently makes time to attend conferences and events where he can enjoy this passion and strengthen his leadership skills at the same time. While Scott attended a recent conference for entrepreneurial companies, he had dinner with a fellow member of a coaching program to which he belongs. The other coach has a similar passion for learning about entrepreneurship, and they genuinely hit it off.

After chatting for a while about the speakers, the coach mentioned that he really should be asking Scott about Cornerstone Wealth and what it does. It turned out the coach needed a wealth manager to handle his family's assets, which turned out to be very sizable. They are now discussing the possibility of working together. The conversation would not have happened if Scott had not allowed himself to build his business around his passions.

"To create a workplace where you love to be, it is essential to find people with aligned interests and develop a culture that supports where you are going. We both hire for attitude and then train for skills. Making deposits in the emotional buckets of your team members on a regular basis is also one of the best investments you can make in growing your firm."

So, if you want your Passion that Pays to remain just that—a passion—you must surround yourself with passionate people. That is especially important when building your team. To create a workplace where you love to be, it is essential to find people with aligned interests and develop a culture that supports where you are going. We both hire for attitude and then train for skills. Making deposits in the emotional buckets of your team members on a regular basis is also one of the best investments you can make in growing your firm. One way Ron's company keeps people excited about coming to work is by holding fun events ranging from office golf tournaments to a getaway for elite performers and their spouses every year. Bring Your Dog to Work Day is probably the most popular. When one top recruit was choosing between an offer from Carson Wealth and another firm, seeing a notice about that event told her that Ron's firm's culture was right for her. This can be done in a small firm, too. Every quarter, Scott's firm holds a lively celebration, such as a bowling tournament with trophies for the winners (and losers), or he takes his team skeet shooting. Maintaining a strong culture of passion in your own way will help you attract team members who energize you and free you to do what you are best at.

Define Your Core Competency

To reach your full potential as a leader, you must understand your core competency and that of your firm. Core competency is what you do best and at what you're most competitive. Personally, it energizes you and gives you joy. Your core competency is something you'd do even if you weren't paid to do it. Knowing your core competency will help simplify your complex world into one basic, organizing idea. It will enable you to focus yourself and your company on achieving one or, at most, a few big goals. Knowing your core competency and tapping into it is the key to achieving the Sustainable Edge.

"Knowing your core competency and tapping into it is the key to achieving the Sustainable Edge."

We should point out that your core competency isn't only about building a career around what you enjoy doing. Many people fail at businesses built around their favorite hobby or passion. Your core competency must be a value creator for you and the people you serve. The key to building a great business lies in turning your passions into productivity—remember, it's your Passion that Pays.

> *"The key to building a great business lies in turning your passions into productivity, creating your Passion that Pays."*

One clue to identifying your core competency is knowing what people are willing to pay you a big premium to do for them. Think of the best golf pro you've ever met. Not only are they great at golf, which is likely their passion, they are also good instructors. Thus, they are turning their passion into productivity, creating a Passion that pays. Is there an example like this in your life—something you love doing that you can capitalize on?

Knowing your core competency will help you focus your energy and resources in the right direction. It will guide you to the right decisions in every key area of your business. On a recent hunting trip, one of Scott's friends, a veterinarian involved in global philanthropy, downplayed his deep expertise. He claimed that all he knew was "having a knife in my hand and doing surgery." He thought he ought to broaden his horizons. But, from Scott's point of view, his intense focus is what helped him to unlock his genius and become a great veterinarian.

In 2006, Ron's firm had the opportunity to invest in a large car dealership. His company had plenty of cash on hand, and the deal looked great on paper. But as Ron dug into the details, his gut instinct told him not to bite. Running car dealerships is not Carson Wealth's core competency. It was easy to see the project devouring Carson Wealth's time and resources, which would be better spent on what the firm does best, so Ron passed on the deal.

As you might have guessed, it was the right move. Within a few years of passing on the deal, the dealership filed for bankruptcy protection. As Ron looks back at the "opportunity" now, he finds it to be a great reminder why you should focus on what you do best, especially when you are pursuing the Sustainable Edge. Recognizing (and accepting) that managing an automotive dealership was outside of his firm's expertise saved Carson Wealth an enormous amount of time, money, and energy.

With exponentially increasing competition in today's market, it is more important than ever for entrepreneurs to focus on their core competency. You must know, definitively, where you can add value to the marketplace—and you must act on it every day. It is better to excel in one niche than to try to be good at everything, if you want to achieve the Sustainable Edge. Practice your core competency until you can execute it flawlessly. Intense focus is the key to harnessing the power of your mind to achieve success. If you try to improve on all of your weaknesses, you'll end up with quite a few strong weaknesses and underdeveloped strengths. We're sure you've never complimented someone on their underdeveloped strengths! Tap into your core competency as if you were a star athlete—then you'll never have to rethink it in the moment and risk "choking."

Google is a great example of excelling in one niche. From day one, it committed itself to being the best and most used online search tool and devoted its every resource to dominating its market. What search engine do you use? We're pretty confident that if you tried any others, you'd see that no one else comes close to what Google offers. By honing in on its niche, Google has become the go-to search engine. In fact, its name brand has even become the verb we use to describe searching the Internet.

Amazon is another example of a company that excels in listening to its customers. Responding to customer frustration with "wrap rage," the experience of becoming angry and frustrated with, even cutting yourself on, excessive packaging, Jeff Bezos invested in a multi-year initiative to develop frustration-free packaging. The company now delivers shipments in easy-to-open recyclable boxes without a lot of excess plastic and other packing materials in the box.

If it's not possible for you to be the best in your particular category, you may have to invent a new category, just as Al Ries and Jack Trout explain in the *22 Immutable Laws of Marketing*. Ries and Trout tell the story of Avis Car Rental, which realized it could never be the biggest auto rental firm with Hertz in the picture. Enlisting the help of DDB Worldwide Communications Group—which asked "Why would anyone rent cars from Avis?"—it came up with the tagline "We try harder." That tagline was drawn directly from the company's answer to the question, and it has now guided the Avis mission for fifty years.

Lose focus on your core competency and your business ventures will suffer. One of Ron's clients ran fifty businesses in roofing, irrigation, siding, document storage—you name it—when they first began their working relationship. To pull off running so many businesses, the entrepreneur had almost as many different partners. Ron wondered how he could keep track of everything. Well, he couldn't. His life was a mess, and he certainly wasn't enjoying it. He finally sold everything but his roofing business—his original company and the one he valued most. Once he focused on it, his life became much simpler. Growth in his roofing business exploded, and he was able to achieve the Sustainable Edge.

Ron's client got caught in a common trap for entrepreneurs—chasing the next shiny object that you think will grow your firm. We've been guilty of this as well and have learned from our mistakes. In 2003, Ron's firm invested in software called Breaking Away. At the time, the venture looked promising. It gradually became apparent that the software project was beyond the firm's core competency and was going to cost much more than anyone predicted. In 2010, Carson Wealth ended up selling the business for less than the firm had invested. In retrospect, the software's name might be seen as a red flag, signaling to the firm that they should break away from the project.

———

To keep his firm tightly focused, Ron now sets a Most Vital for Carson Wealth's year ahead. It reinforces the firm's goal of embracing its niche. He reminds his team members to keep the firm's mission statement and how they fit into it at the top of their minds.

The Carson Wealth team has taken him seriously. About a decade ago, Ron suggested that Carson Wealth provide travel agency services to help its clients plan vacations. In his enthusiasm, he ignored the reality that it didn't fit into the firm's core competency. Then someone on his operations team courageously spoke up. "Can you tell me how that fits into our mission statement?" she asked. Ron was a little embarrassed that he couldn't answer the question definitively, but he felt proud he'd empowered his team to challenge him. Avoiding a detour into travel services undoubtedly saved the firm a lot of time and money.

As we've both realized, there's no silver bullet to growth. But we have figured out that the quickest route is knowing what you do best and continually finding ways to do it better. Saying no to pursuits that distract you from your Passion that Pays will allow you the space, time, and energy to accomplish more than you ever dreamed.

For the entrepreneurial minded, opportunities seem to be around every corner. Don't be afraid to get into serious and critical exploration of what you can realistically accomplish on a world-class level so that you choose the right opportunity. In 2009, Scott's team spent two days debating what would differentiate Cornerstone Wealth from its competition. His team believed delivering excellent service was the answer. Scott decided that they were right—his firm could compete at the highest levels in service—but he kept returning to innovation as what really stirs his passion.

> *"Keep your core competency as narrowly focused as possible, and you'll stay on track."*

When Carson Wealth revisited the issue in 2012, the landscape had changed. Scott had joined Ron's Carson Institutional Alliance (CIA), which was designed to enable elite advisors to offer their clients better service and more cutting-edge technology than they could afford to do on their own. By joining CIA, Scott set himself up to finally compete at the highest level in innovation, where his energy and enthusiasm have always been. Today, Cornerstone Wealth's core competency is innovating. It only took an hour of debate for Scott to persuade his team that the new focus on innovation would help improve customer service. That's how clear he was in his intention. Engaging in the process of getting feedback, as Scott did, is critical, so that you can be sure you don't become swept up in the enthusiasm of the moment. It's also important for gaining buy-in from your team. In Scott's case, every one on his team is enthusiastically on board with their new focus on innovation.

Embrace Your Core Competency

We recommend that you ask yourself if you are focused on your core competency once a year. Consider the values, passions, and goals you listed in the IQ Grower™ process.

Now ask yourself a key question. On most days, do the activities on your Essential Six and Most Vital connect directly to what you value, what makes you happy, and your most important goals? If not, you're seeing the sign that you and your firm may be working outside of your core competency.

Many entrepreneurs are so busy they have a hard time keeping track of how they spend their time. Or, perhaps, they are not being honest with themselves about what they're filling their days with. If you're among them, we urge you to try an experiment. Set an alarm to ring every fifteen minutes. Write down what you have been doing for each of the intervals. Are you spending your time focused on and working toward achieving your most important goals? If you are not, ask yourself what you can do to sync up your time with your goals. Make a game plan to free up the hours you are wasting on activities that drain you or don't support your bigger goals.

Of course, we know you're dealing in reality here. Some activities that drain you are a means to an end. For instance, if you are an introvert, meeting with clients or interviewing potential hires may exhaust you. But if you look at those tasks as steps toward growing your firm, they may become invigorating. Tackling them is like hiking to the top of the mountain. It's difficult, but the closer your steps get you to the peak, the faster you will get there.

Not long ago, Ron was scaling a peak in Colorado. He got to thinking about the values exercise within the IQ Grower™ process. As he considered his own values, he thought about a conversation he had with his wife the night before his hike. Jeanie had mentioned that they should begin attending church services again. But Ron didn't want to go. He thought about how disappointed his wife would be if she knew that he could not list faith as one of his top values. Ron's mother is agnostic, and his father is atheist. Ron, himself, is a very spiritual person, but he has always struggled with organized religion. As he neared the peak of the fourteener—a mountain taller than 14,000 feet—he discovered a group of thirty people. On a normal hike, there might be ten people at most enjoying the view.

As he took in the scene, Ron saw a priest, clothed in robes and standing at an altar, delivering Mass. Father John Nepil noticed Ron and invited him to stay.

"Father, I'm not Catholic," Ron said.

"It doesn't matter. Just listen for a few minutes," Father Nepil said. "If you're not compelled to stay, then you can leave."

"As much as I'd love to stay, I'm a little worried about the weather," Ron told him. The clouds were starting to build, indicating a potential snowstorm.

"I've done this peak before," the priest said. "I know a different way down. It won't take us long."

Ron stayed. Standing on the peak in the beauty of nature at 14,000 feet, it was almost as if he received a personal message from heaven saying "We're here." He had never felt so close to God. It was a surreal moment in which he found new insight into his faith and a greater understanding of God and the world around him. He was able to see and accept the possibility that he may have misunderstood faith. If the experience had not occurred on the mountaintop, he might have thought Jeanie had contrived it to happen.

Just as Ron suspected, bad weather arrived and just as Mass was ending. In the bad conditions, it was impossible to see more than five feet ahead and the descent was slow and difficult going with the group of young college students—inexperienced climbers—who had attended the service. The priest enlisted Ron's help to guide them down the peak safely. If Ron had not been an experienced mountaineer, the group would have surely been in trouble. Talk about being in the right place at the right time.

In another right-place-right-time experience not long ago, Ron was planning a bird hunt to benefit his Dreamweaver Foundation (thedreamweaverfoundation.org), a charity dedicated to fulfilling end-of-life dreams for impoverished seniors with terminal illnesses. Ron's personal goal is to build Dreamweaver's assets to $1 billion, to ensure that it becomes and remains a sustainable endeavor. He was planning to auction tickets to the hunt during the upcoming holiday season. While he was working on plans for the upcoming holiday hunt, he happened to meet the head basketball coach at the University of Nebraska. Ron's subconscious offered a brilliant idea at the precise moment he could make the most of it. In Nebraska, basketball coaches are celebrities. If the coach—an avid bird hunter—were the official hunt host, bidders at the auction would bid five times more than the starting ticket price to attend the bird hunt. The coach agreed to help, allowing Ron to reach his goal to raise funds for the foundation even faster.

Whether it is a spiritual belief or a business opportunity, your mind must be prepared to receive the clarity of vision that may arrive unexpectedly. When you are in a frame of mind to absorb them, they can become a powerful guiding light. If Ron had not been in the midst of reviewing his values, he probably would have arrived at top of the peak, taken in the view, and headed back down. Committing to the IQ Grower™ process will keep you ready to receive powerful messages from your subconscious that will help you achieve a richer life.

The Power of No

Most success in business comes from what you say no to. The more you free your time to say yes to the parts of your business where you excel, the more profitable your business will be. The Essential Six and Most Vital exercises are critical to helping you say yes to the right questions. The exercises remind you to focus first on what is most significant to lead your company, so you can reach your big goals. Equally important, the exercises weed out those tasks or projects that will waste your time.

A mission statement will guide your company the same way, so you make the right business decisions. Mission statements give direction and purpose for an entire organization and provide a filter as to what is important and what is not.

As you scale up your firm, sticking with your core competency may require you to branch out into areas where you're above average, but maybe not the best in the world. For instance, Carson Wealth's core competency is wealth management. But Ron has added ancillary services like tax planning and preparation as a convenience for his clients. Does that seem to violate the principle of doing a select few things at a world-class level? It doesn't if you agree that the firm's core competency is client experience. In Ron's case, offering extras like tax planning and preparation fits seamlessly. It makes Carson Wealth's client experience world class.

It can be difficult to know if a new business focus will complement your value proposition or become a total distraction. Encourage your team to be honest about debating it and whether it fits your core competency. Otherwise, it will be very easy to follow many diverging paths and justify ideas that you may regret later. Chasing a big paycheck or quick money can throw you off course. It will keep you busy, but you will lose the important element of balance.

If you keep your core competency as narrowly focused as possible, you'll stay on track. It will bring you—and your whole team—clarity and help you achieve the Sustainable Edge.

Keep Yourself Honest

Do you want to know if you have identified your core competency correctly and are executing on it? Your customer is the ultimate judge and jury. In their classic *Harvard Business Review* article, "Customer Intimacy and Other Value Disciplines," Michael Treacy and Fred Wiersema explain how companies like Dell, Home Depot, and Nike grew from small ideas to crush their competitors. These companies did three things:

1. They redefined value for customers.

2. They built powerful business systems that delivered more of that value.

3. They raised customers' expectations beyond what rivals could achieve.

To achieve those goals in your own firm, there is no substitute for requesting feedback from your clientele. Put a mechanism in place to hold yourself accountable for what you are delivering to customers. We recommend forming a client advisory council of your target customers. When you are trying to allocate limited resources, they can help you rank what is most important to pursue.

"Customers are your ultimate judge and jury when it comes to your core competency. Putting systems in place to collect their feedback will keep you honest."

Customers are your ultimate judge and jury when it comes to your core competency. Putting systems in place to collect their feedback will keep you honest. For example, Scott's firm uses the Net Promoter Score and System, an objective measure of how likely customers are to refer his firm to others. You might be familiar with the NPS System, which "provides a best practice framework for how companies collect, evaluate, and act on customer feedback to optimize financial benefits" (http://www.netpromoter.com/why-net-promoter/know/). Asking directly for feedback is a powerful tool as well. When Ron held his first staff retreat, he asked a customer to talk with his team about what Carson Wealth was great at. "I really like you, Ron—I don't want to hurt your feelings—but you guys are pretty average at everything," his client said.

That bucket of ice water woke Ron up. At the time, he believed his firm to be excelling in most areas. He returned from the meeting and immediately implemented a client advisory council that still exists as a vital component of his feedback system. This group has helped him to answer some fundamental questions: If I want to keep you as a client, what do I have to deliver? Am I delivering what I think I am delivering? In what category can I really dominate? Many of Carson Wealth's best practices today—from the way it opens meetings to its trade notes—flowed out of recommendations the counsel has made.

Even offhand comments from clients can be valuable. One of Ron's clients who moved out of the Omaha area mentioned that she felt she was missing out on client-education events at Carson Wealth's headquarters. Realizing that other distant clients might feel the same way, the firm began to offer virtual meetings.

If you're not getting feedback from your customers, it's because you're not asking for it. Business owners must stay ahead of what customers like and don't like and how their business can improve. It's also essential to ask for feedback from internal stakeholders and to weave those requests into your meeting rhythms and structure. Internal stakeholders are often the first to spot pockets of opportunity or areas where clients are becoming dissatisfied. Tap into the best ideas of your clients and your internal team members, and you will be well on your way to achieving the Sustainable Edge. Ron often says, "At Carson Wealth we believe in associates. We refer to our employees as stakeholders. When we hire our associates, we tell them working here is a life sentence, but in a good way. We say that, because we want them to know they are valued from day one, and we want them to see working here as a career, not a job."

"At Carson Wealth we believe in associates. We refer to our employees as stakeholders. When we hire our associates, we tell them working here is a life sentence, but in a good way. We say that, because we want them to know they are valued from day one, and we want them to see working here as a career, not a job."

IQ Grower™ Exercises to Identify Your Passion that Pays

Can you envision wealth as it relates to your passions?

Revisit your personal core competencies. Review them closely and think about how they align to you your firm's core competencies. Are there any that need adjusting?

Imagine dialing in on your true goals—both in business and in your personal life. What actions can you take to make your goals a reality?

Can you use your core competency to lead you toward that special niche in the marketplace where you will be seen as exceptional? If so, how will you go about it? What about this core competency will set you apart from others and how can you build on that?

When you hear the word exceptional in regard to your business, what do you see? What steps can you take that vision a reality?

Resource Link

Identifying and Developing Strengths:

http://www.strengthsfinder.com

4.

HONE YOUR FIRM'S MAIN THING

There is no magic ticket to growth. The quickest route is by identifying what you do best and continuing to find ways to do it better. Saying no to pursuits that distract you from your focus will allow you to accomplish more than you ever dreamed. Setting one clear annual goal—your company's "Main Thing"—makes it much easier to do that. It will help you explain your goals to your team and rally everyone around it. Your Main Thing should reflect where your value lies for your clients. It is your commitment, based on your company's mission statement, and how you are going to deliver on that mission. In your daily life, using the Essential Six and Most Vital will help you support your firm's Main Thing.

At many firms, the Main Thing for the year is to move the needle on a key performance indicator such as revenue, profits, or the company's Net Promoter Score. At Scott's firm, for instance, the annual goal is to attract a specific amount of new assets under management. Scott's team debates its Main Thing at an annual strategic planning event that usually lasts a day or two. All of his team members get to be the CEO for the day and say what they think the Main Thing for the year should be before they make any final decisions.

> "The quickest route to growth is through identifying what you do best and continuing to find ways to do it better."

Clarify Your Values

Small and midsize firms cannot dominate a giant category; they must occupy the right niche. Maybe you can't be number one in size, but you can be the best in trust, transparency, and accountability, which are the core values and drivers of Carson Wealth and Cornerstone Wealth.

> "Maybe you can't be number one in size, but you can be the best in trust, transparency, and accountability."

You are probably already familiar with the classic Strengths, Weaknesses, Opportunities, and Threats (SWOT) analysis. It can get you off to a great start in identifying your niche. However, your niche should not only reflect market realities. Your values must come into play, too, if you want to identify your Main Thing. The following exercises will help connect the two. They may seem abstract and challenging, but if you dig deep and persevere the answers will come.

1. What category can you create for your business that encompasses and transcends your values? _____

   _____

   _____

2. What brings you meaning and for what are you grateful?

   _____

   _____

3. Consider your personal values and elevate them to the forefront of your actions, just as Ron did with his dedication to the Dreamweaver Foundation. He built this organization as a direct result of the IQ Grower™ exercises. What opportunities can you seize by aligning your values with your actions? _____

   _____

   _____

Multiply Your Firm's Value

Committing to your Main Thing is more than a technique to manage your team's time and resources. It will also greatly increase the value of your business. One of Ron's clients sold his firm to a Fortune

100 firm recently. In the six months leading up to the sale, the business owner settled on one Main Thing—to maximize the valuation of the firm. In order to accomplish that, he made it a goal to make sure the team saved as much money and it was as profitable as it could be. It is much easier to sell a business for a high valuation if buyers understand exactly what it does and where it excels.

Holding a contest where internal stakeholders could compete for prizes, the client got the company's 400-member team excited about slashing spending. Whoever submitted the top three ideas would win. As the entries poured in, it was eye opening for everyone to see how much extraneous spending existed—everywhere from the company's phone system to the health insurance plan. As a result of the internal team stakeholder efforts to trim the budget, the company improved its base earnings by more than $1 million. Ron's client got a seven times multiple on that one million in savings, meaning the exercise resulted in increasing the value of the firm by $7 million.

Sometimes, focusing on your Main Thing requires you to slow down temporarily, so you can speed up your firm's growth later. For instance, at Carson Wealth, Ron and his team set an annual goal for 2014—to create a compliance model for the firm that can be scaled, monitored, and enforced. Ron wanted the firm to achieve an "A" rating or higher, as measured by an outside audit firm. That goal won't "move the needle" financially in the immediate future, but it will ensure that the needle stays in place. It will also help the firm maintain trust, transparency, and accountability—factors that are absolutely critical to its value proposition as a brand and to its clients as it continues to scale.

Sizzle vs. Substance

Your Main Thing should balance sizzle and substance. In our field, it's easy to deliver a lot of sizzle to clients during a bull market, but that alone doesn't result in the Sustainable Edge. You must be sure you can deliver substance, in the form of excellent wealth management, even in a bear market, too. Of course, you have to deliver some sizzle. If you bring great value but no one knows about your firm, you'll go out of business.

> *"Sizzle alone won't result in the Sustainable Edge; you must deliver substance."*

As a company owner, it's easy to "drink your own Kool-Aid" when you get excited about a new Main Thing. To avoid wasting a year going down the wrong path, ask your leadership team for a reality check. Better yet, ask them what your Main Thing should be. Ron typically poses this question to his team at their annual planning meeting, "If you were president for the day, what ideas would you like to see on the table?" No idea is considered irrelevant. That way everyone has equity in the group's success. Aim to be both a truth giver and a truth receiver when you conduct your discussion. Allow your team to be heard and make them feel safe to express their views and debate the ideas under consideration. That requires some vulnerability as a leader. If you tend to be a take-charge, action-oriented personality, you may need to make a few attempts before you get it right, so you don't mow everyone over. At the same time, it's important to keep discussions from getting stuck in nitpicking, or you'll suffer from inertia. We both ask our teams to critique freely but insist they come prepared with solutions to any problems they spot.

Create Your Roadmap

Once you arrive at your annual goal, you will need to put specific, actionable plans into place to support it.

Super Thursday, a program that Ron's firm initiated, has been a powerful magnet for clients and supported CMW's goal of enhancing trust, transparency, and accountability. On the last Thursday of every month, the firms in the Carson Institutional alliance open their doors to the public, prospects, clients, and the media to let these observers see what they are doing behind the scenes each day. One new client transferred $2.4 million from another advisor to Carson Wealth after attending the event. When she asked her former advisor why his firm didn't hold educational events like Super Thursday, his answer was simply, "We don't do that." You can imagine that she was not happy with that response. Another client transferred $24 million in assets because of Carson Wealth's transparency. This client, a trust formed in the 1920s with 104 voting beneficiaries, had to hold a vote to fire their previous wealth management firm in order for Carson Wealth to take over. Ron was astounded that Super Thursdays were becoming so instrumental to his firm's winning new business.

––––––

As we mentioned, Cornerstone Wealth's Main Thing for 2014 was to attract a specific, measurable total of new assets under management. Scott planned to accomplish this both organically and through acquisitions. To support that goal, Carson Institutional Alliance ramped up the firm's marketing plan and introduced a new technology called the Client Experience Optimizer.

Cornerstone Wealth sets four quarterly goals to underpin its annual goal. During the third quarter of 2014, for instance, the firm's quarterly goal was focused on marketing. To achieve that goal, Scott's team made it a top priority to participate in Carson Wealth's Super Thursday. Since his conference room comfortably seats fifteen guests, he invites that many prospects and key clients to meet with his advisors. His goal is to connect with and retain clients who are an ideal fit for the firm.

Not long ago, Scott invited clients to attend a Super Thursday presentation to help deepen the relationship with the firm. After they attended, Scott was confident that his clients appreciated the added value. Even more recently, he invited a local insurance agency owner. After attending just one Super Thursday, not only did I feel this prospect would refer clients to me, but also that he would ask me to manage his money. When you are getting results like this, you will know your plans are on the right track.

Accountability and Rewards Matter

The best way to make sure you achieve your annual and quarterly goals is to establish clear accountability and rewards for achieving them. At Carson Wealth, Ron's team sets its key goals at an annual retreat. The leadership team discusses and debates what is most critical to accomplish and does a SWOT analysis on the company's goals. Finally, the executive committee votes to set priorities. Once these are decided, the firm assigns a champion who is in charge of reporting, on a monthly and quarterly basis, to the leadership team on the company's progress in meeting the goals. Each month there is a celebration, like a bowling night, to mark the firm's progress.

> "The best way to make sure you achieve your annual and quarterly goals is to establish clear accountability and rewards for achieving them."

To underline your commitment to a goal, tie your team's compensation to meeting a benchmark. Ron's firm pays semiannual bonuses. His firm utilizes a scorecard process to make sure his team members know where they stand and can catch up if they're falling behind.

In 2013, Ron's firm decided it was important to emphasize the client experience above all as its Main Thing. To meet its goal, the firm had recently staffed up, but service levels were declining according to an internal measure it uses to keep tabs on client satisfaction. With more team members, there was more room for error. Instead of tying a portion of its team's bonuses to hitting revenue targets, Carson Wealth linked them to achieving a 25 percent improvement in productivity. Not having properly integrated, repeatable policies and procedures was hurting his team's efficiency. By fixing that problem, Ron knew the firm would improve the customer experience, resulting in higher customer satisfaction scores. That would be a huge long-term win for the firm.

Focusing most of its energy on improving productivity in order to improve client satisfaction in 2013, Carson Wealth achieved an 84 percent improvement in productivity in just fifteen months. That was more than three times its goal. The firm's customer-satisfaction scores are now back to where they were before the firm scaled up, and there has been a dramatic improvement in direct feedback from clients.

More importantly, Ron has gotten Carson Wealth to a place where he can honestly say his team never loses focus on its Main Thing. It is incorporated into digital dashboards and discussed constantly at meetings, so it always remains top of mind. Every morning, his leadership team has a quick check-in meeting where everyone shares an update on what they are doing to support the Main Thing. They also discuss the one task or goal they need help accomplishing. He supports them by refraining from adding big jobs to their plate until the Main Thing is accomplished. Ron's accountability to his team and their accountability to the firm's Main Thing is why his firm is growing so fast.

So can yours.

IQ Grower™ Exercises to Hone Your Firm's Main Thing

What is the one thing you can focus on for the year and next quarter that will have the biggest impact on your company?

Do a SWOT analysis: http://www.quickmba.com/strategy/swot.

What are you hearing from internal and external stakeholders?

What should you stop doing and why?

Resource Link

https://www.gazelles.com/static/resources/tools/en/growth -tools-all.pdf

5.

CREATE YOUR BRAIN TRUST TO BENEFIT FROM THE BEST AND THE BRIGHTEST

The XPRIZE Foundation inspires hundreds of the brightest minds on the planet to tackle the seemingly unsolvable problems facing humanity—like extracting clean drinking water from the sea to offset our water use. Run by pioneering aerospace entrepreneur Peter Diamandis, it offers multimillion-dollar prizes to entice teams to compete in its competitions. Ultimately, the foundation challenges XPRIZE winners to produce a return of at least ten times the value of the prize and to spark at least 100 times the follow-on investment and social benefit.

Imagine if you could tap the same global pool of brainpower to multiply the growth of your business and achieve the Sustainable

Edge—even if you didn't have millions of dollars to offer as a bounty. Smart people around the globe—or even in your own community—would help you see what you need to stay competitive, take advantage of market shifts, and stay in sync with customers. You would reduce your risk of being blindsided by competitors who do things better, faster, and for less money. Salim Ismail describes this in his recent book, *Exponential Organizations*. Ismail, cofounder of Singularity University with Diamandis, is a Silicon Valley organization that teaches leaders how to use exponential technologies to solve problems.

The good news is you can bring exponential thinking to your organization without offering a multimillion-dollar prize or engaging a Silicon Valley think tank by forming your "Brain Trust." We've based this process on Napoleon Hill's concept of the Mastermind Alliance, which he presented in *Think and Grow Rich*. Hill encouraged entrepreneurs to bring together a group of peers to share and workshop ideas in a confidential setting. Today, digital connectivity tools such as LinkedIn and Twitter make it possible to take that idea to a level beyond Hill's. Through this process of reaching out—whether within your boardroom or LinkedIn group—you will solicit an everevolving group of business owners who help you identify blind spots and potential liabilities, test predictions so you can stay ahead of the changes affecting your customers and your culture, and achieve a minimum of 15 percent annual growth. Ask smart questions in the right way, and you can easily mine ideas from exceptional colleagues around the world without ever adding them to your staff.

some wealth managers fear will displace them. Ron has no objection to letting Steve see what Carson Wealth is doing and sharing its best practices, because that means Ron's firm will, in turn, be able to learn from what Betterment is doing. In fact, the Carson Group of companies is considering offering its clients Betterment as a small account solution. Both Ron and Steve know that both Carson Wealth and Betterment share a commitment to bringing more value to the consumer and that it's healthy for their industry if they exchange great ideas that elevate their profession. This concept of emphasizing value to the customer above all else was pioneered by John Bogle, founder and retired CEO of The Vanguard Group and author of the book *Enough*, a book Ron and Scott consider to be one of the most influential reads of their careers.

Many of the more than 1,100 advisors in the Peak Advisor Alliance (PAA), Ron's coaching program, have embraced a similar approach. These business owners bring their own ideas and their colleagues with ideas to the table. Ron is amazed by how much sharing and caring goes on when he attends his PAA's Excel conferences and witnesses firsthand how much learning is shared among industry thought leaders. Everyone is trying to make each other better and stronger, even though many of them are competitors in the same markets. They know it will help them collectively as the profession advances. To expand the pool of customers it taps, Carson Wealth will add two new advisory councils, representing millennial and women customers, in 2015. These groups will also become part of his Brain Trust.

> *"It only takes a few minutes to tap into the wisdom of the best minds in the world or to mine big data."*

It only takes a few minutes to tap into the wisdom of the best minds in the world or to mine big data. Make it an essential part of the fifteen minutes a week you dedicate to the IQ Grower™ exercises. Often, when you reach out beyond your immediate circle, you'll come across amazing information you might never have discovered. It's the same principle used on the show *Who Wants to Be a Millionaire?* As you may recall from this show, asking the audience often leads to the best answer.

So how do you build your Brain Trust to help you achieve the 15 percent minimum growth you need to achieve the Sustainable Edge?

Discover Your Ideal Advisors

To build your Brain Trust, it is important to identify the most significant challenges to your goals and objectives. Your Brain Trust should include people with the expertise to help you tackle them. To identify them, make a list of the people who know what you need to find out, who care about your success, and who are not a competitive threat to you. Start from the inside of your organization or the people closest to you and build outward. Don't miss out on the value of tapping into groups, clubs, foundations, support groups, and organizations that add to the quality of your Brain Trust. Selecting them carefully will greatly expand the pool of great minds you bring into your orbit.

> "Selecting your Brain Trust carefully will greatly expand the pool of great minds you bring into your orbit."

This first group will include your internal stakeholders, because they are intimately involved in running your business. At Cornerstone Wealth, for instance, at the close of each weekly meeting Scott asks his team what the firm should start, stop, and continue doing. By engaging in this practice, he gets valuable feedback on how he can improve the firm's operations in mere minutes.

Asking for direct feedback from clients is also critical. When Scott noticed his firm's Net Promoter Score was slipping, primarily from out-of-town customers, he contacted several to ask what was wrong. The customers didn't have a specific complaint but mentioned they'd be more comfortable working with an advisor in their own local area. To improve the firm's relationship with its long-distance clients, Scott enhanced his firm's GoToMeeting capabilities and added a button on his website that offers a "Virtual meeting with Scott Ford."

To tap into your Sustainable Edge, we encourage you to take efforts like this a step further to connect with experts in the digital realm, too. Make a list of social media outlets to which you can commit and how you will use them. Perhaps you want to spark

discussions in a LinkedIn group, for instance. Consider other you will use as well. Video is very important and accounts growing percentage of web traffic—our brains absorb inform more easily from images than from the written word, so ther reason not to harness the power of video.

USE A THREE-TIERED APPROACH

We recommend a three-tiered approach to creating your Br Trust, which should include formal advisors connected to yo firm, peers from outside the firm, and smart people you meet social media. You may also want to include experts whose ide. you hear at events. Every six months, for instance, Scott attend a growth conference run by Gazelles, an executive education firm for midmarket companies. Gazelles events present thought leaders who share the best ideas from their recently published best-selling books. So, over a two-day period, Scott is able to learn from some of the best minds in the world every six months as well as learning from the other attendees.

Ron used the three-tiered approach to set up his Brain Trust. One key part is an advisory council for Carson Wealth made up of clients and important people of influence who give him regular feedback. Ron is a big believer in inviting competition to the table, rather than taking a guarded approach to rivals. For example, one of the board members at Carson Wealth, Steve Lockshin, is an investor in Betterment Institutional, the automated investing service that

Outside his firm, Ron gets advice from peers in three Young Presidents' Organization (YPO) chapters. YPO is a global, invitation-only network of chief executives from a variety of different industries that offers confidential forums where they can share ideas. Ron meets with one of his YPO groups, to which he has belonged since 1994, for a half-day every month. There are always one or two presentations where members share information on "needs and leads," asking the other members for help with key goals. Not only do they share with each other but they also become important connectors for each other. In addition, members can call an emergency meeting at any time if they have a business or personal issue they need help with. Ron attends YPO's annual retreat, where he deepens these essential personal and professional relationships. The other two YPO chapters to which Ron belongs are made up of financial services professionals, bringing him into contact with fresh, industry-specific ideas on a semiannual basis.

Make the Most of Social Media

Using social media, like LinkedIn and Twitter, the members of Ron's YPO groups stay connected even when they are not meeting in person. Beyond keeping in touch with his in-person network, Ron and Scott use social media to make new connections that will help his business grow. They have promoted their blogs on Twitter and LinkedIn to position themselves as a thought leaders in their areas of expertise and to connect with new customers and prospects. They also send out relevant news and information bites on Twitter to their followers, which drives a considerable portion of the firms' traffic to their websites. For instance, when he got the news that Carson Wealth had been selected for the Barron's Hall of Fame in the fall of 2014, Ron shared that update immediately with his Twitter followers. Then his firm embarked on a large-scale campaign to spread the news through blogs and LinkedIn.

The results of such efforts are sometimes surprising. Not long ago, Ron shared some photos from a bird hunt on Twitter. One of his followers, also an avid bird hunter, saw them and mentioned he would be traveling from Minneapolis to Omaha soon. They ended up meeting in person recently, and, given their joint passion for birds, they had much to share in conversation. He is exactly the type of prospect who is ideal for Ron's business, and they continue to stay in touch. Ron uses LinkedIn in a variety of ways. One of the most powerful uses has been to reconnect with business contacts. Ron rolled out his Digital Fortress™ program after reconnecting with a former associate who is now our technical partner, which offers a cutting-edge, content-delivery platform. At the time, Ron's firm had been embarking on a different development path to change the way Carson Wealth delivered content. Within a week of reconnecting through the site, Craig flew to Omaha to present his ideas with Ron. As a result, Carson Wealth made a complete 180 on its approach to content delivery. Had it not been for LinkedIn, Carson Wealth would have continued using its legacy platform, instead of moving to the more revolutionary one it uses now. The firm is now much better positioned today to grow and scale its coaching and consulting business because of this relationship made as a result of LinkedIn. It's important to note that Ron is a regular user of both Twitter and LinkedIn, the social network with the widest acceptance among professionals. If you cannot maintain an active presence on your social media sites, you may not see great results. He has 7,000 LinkedIn followers and participates in a 2,600-person discussion group run by LPL Financial.

In another situation, a former high-level executive of TD Ameritrade connected with Ron through LinkedIn. Now they are working together on a cutting-edge risk assessment software that Ron's firm and prospects will be able to use through his company's website.

Sometimes, Ron actively poses questions to the online groups in which he is a member. Other times, he simply "lurks" in the background, paying attention to relevant discussions. He will also engage in "passion prospecting"—chatting with fellow users in the hope that he will discover some who share his appreciation of fine wine, aviation, and football and who may need his firm's services down the road. He never expects to "sell" someone through social media. It is more of a way to get acquainted, start building a relationship, and move the conversation down the road to the point it makes sense to set up a phone call or meeting.

Developing and maintaining a consistent message on social media is essential when you are trying to reach prospects, advises Jimmy Williams, a wealth manager at Compass Capital Management in Oklahoma, who is a member of PAA, Ron's coaching program.

"Our success with social media is based on consistency, frequency, and follow-up," Jimmy says.

> Many business owners think daily or hourly posting is necessary to be noticed and attract prospects. We believe that's the wrong mindset! By posting high-quality, engaging information that rises above the noises of messages in the daily newsfeed, our firm has experienced more success than ever. A fresh, positive, and informative post twice, or maybe three times, per week will generate significant traffic and will define your site as one that is truly meaningful.

Williams says his firm is diligent in following up on requests for information offered in its posts. "This is the most critical of steps to our developing a social media strategy that is both productive and profitable for our firm," he says. It pays off. On an annual basis, his firm's social media profile sites provide the firm with approximately $6 to $10 million in new accounts under management while requiring approximately fifteen minutes per week of his staff, he says.

Using social media effectively and productively isn't a huge investment of time, as Jimmy Williams has proven. The same holds true for Ron. All told, he spends about ten minutes a day managing his social media. To keep sites like LinkedIn from becoming a time suck, Ron makes the most of efficiency boosting technology, like PAA's Digital Fortress, a program that allows business owners to automate their postings across various social media sites. For business owners who don't have time to write blog posts, the platform provides content that has been preapproved to comply with financial industry regulations but can be customized with a personal touch and published. You don't have to take advantage of Digital Fortress. There are a variety of other tools, such as Hootsuite, that can help you make social media manageable for your own business.

Your digital Brain Trust can also help you solve specific problems that come up. That became clear when Ron faced a situation where, when a client passed away, only two out of seventeen beneficiaries remaining met the firm's minimum account size. Ron wanted to win the business of the two that qualified but didn't want to offend the fifteen who didn't. After struggling to find a solution on his own, an advisor Ron met on LinkedIn offered a brilliant suggestion. Rather than impose a minimum account size, why not charge a minimum fee to manage an account? Their advisor's firm charged a $25,000 fee to do so on the premise that beneficiaries with, say, only $1,000 to invest would automatically self-select out of using his firm without feeling insulted. The advisor's idea helped spark one that Ron is now considering—creating a desk that will help serve accounts with assets of $100,000 or less but not provide the services of an advisor. Clients with assets above that amount will pay a minimum fee to work with an advisor. Also, in response to the new idea, Carson Wealth recently embarked on an analysis to determine what that fee should be. Ron learned that accounts would need to contain $115,000 or more for the firm to break even under this new model—a fact that astounds him because, under its old cost structure, Carson Wealth client accounts were required to contain $722,000 in assets for the firm to break even. Better yet, once his firm breaks even the first year, the analysis showed it will make a profit the second year, because labor costs are less, thanks to the firm's use of technologies that work together harmoniously.

Sometimes, the community on LinkedIn can be a good reality check and help you realize there is no right answer to a pressing question, saving you the trip down a rabbit hole. Not long ago, Ron's company was letting go of a senior executive who was not only difficult, he simply did not fit into the rest of the team. Although human resources drafted a letter to the executive, Ron felt it was too generic. So Ron inquired on LinkedIn about the best way to let a team member go. He received many responses. He quickly realized that Carson Wealth's internal team needed to come up with its own unique solution to fit the employee's situation. There was no one perfect answer. While this experience was ultimately helpful for Ron, he cautions that, when using online crowdsourcing and social networking tools, you must sort and filter incoming information effectively, so you don't get overwhelmed or misled.

To get the most out of information you gather, we recommend doing a SWOT analysis on any ideas you plan to pursue. Also consider your sources. Are you dealing with someone who truly wants to help you grow? Or is it possible you are talking to a competitor or someone who is jealous of your success and inclined to give you bad advice? Without the social cues you get in an in-person meeting, it's sometimes difficult to tell. When Ron develops a great idea from his social media sources that he would like to act on, he'll have it further vetted by his internal team. He may also schedule a call with the colleague who suggested it or try to meet them in person.

Some professionals worry that using social media may have negative repercussions. In all his years of active use Ron has never had a problem. The key is prudence. As long as you remember that anything you post on social media will remain there forever, you won't go wrong. At the same time, don't let that reality paralyze you from trying social media. Just put your best foot forward, just as you would at any business gathering, and you'll attract the right advisors to your Brain Trust who will help carry your business to the next level.

It's Your Brain Trust

There's no one right way to build your Brain Trust, so think hard about what help you need and focus on those who can provide the most valuable advice in the time you have available. While Ron finds social media invaluable, Scott is just now incorporating sites like Twitter and LinkedIn into his Brain Trust. In Scott's case, going to conferences, including growth summits for mid-market companies and being part of the PAA, Ron's coaching program, gives him access to ideas from more than a thousand business owners who help him scale his business. He pays close attention to what the larger firms are doing when he attends events and meetings.

The ideas Scott has accessed at Alliance meetings have been invaluable. Like Ron, Scott has been investigating the most customer-friendly ways to charge for his firm's services. At one recent meeting, an advisor mentioned an idea that Scott is now considering—giving customers pricing options that correspond to the level of service they want. For instance, someone who wants to entrust their money to Cornerstone Wealth without taking on an advisor would pay one price, while someone who wants to work with an advisor would pay another.

While we recommend making the most of technology, sometimes low-tech methods are the best way to tap your Brain Trust. Wherever the smartest people in your field show up is where you want to be, so you can fuel your business with the best ideas for growth and achieve the Sustainable Edge. If you put the time into shaping and creating your Brain Trust, it will help you to shape and create your success. This is crucial to achieving the Sustainable Edge.

IQ Grower™ Exercises to Help You Create Your Brain Trust

Make a list of the people with the expertise to help you tackle your most significant challenges. Begin from the inside of your organization or the people closest to you and build outward. Answer the following questions:

- Who knows what you need to find out?

- Who knows about your success?

- Who is not a competitive threat to you?

How do you think you can best discover what your customers think of your company?

How can you ask smart questions in the way that will tap into the most constructive answers? What are those smart questions?

Is your social media presence the best it can be? If not, how can you make it better?

What actions can you take to gain better access to the brightest thought leaders in your industry? Are there events you can attend that you have not prioritized? Are there groups you should join, keeping in mind commitment creep and your time priorities?

What type of research can you do to find out what your customers really think of your firm and its performance? Who would you invite into an advisory group?

Resource Link

Crowdsourcing:

https://hbr.org/2013/04/using-the-crowd-as-an
-innovation-partner/

6.

MEASURE WHAT MATTERS ON YOUR ROAD TO 15 PERCENT GROWTH

When Ron started flying at the age of sixteen, the cockpits of most small planes were very complicated. The weather radar was the size of the bottom of a soda bottle. Today, a plane like the Cessna Citation Sovereign Plus still features small controls, but they have been simplified and pared down, so they are much easier to use. Several different devices monitor the fuel and warn if the plane is getting low, but the pilot only sees the data that he or she needs to complete the mission safely. As a result, flying a plane is much easier now.

Ron finds piloting a plane to be a great metaphor for running a business. We recommend you take a similar approach to the metrics you use to track the progress of your business that the aviation industry did for airplanes—simplify. Focus on the key performance indicators (KPIs) that move the needle for your company's annual and quarterly priorities and post them for all to see, so you can achieve the minimum 15 percent growth imperative that is critical to achieving the Sustainable Edge. Simplifying and streamlining, combined with your laser focus on your goals, will make it much easier to pilot your business.

Don't get mired down in tracking too many metrics. Remember, we're encouraging you to simplify. If an activity doesn't provide greater value for your customers and culture in a major way, monitoring it will become a distraction in today's complex business environment. Every metric you use should ultimately contribute to growing your firm at 15 percent or more annually or to contribute factors that indirectly support your goals, such as making your client experience better. The current, number one key performance indicator at Ron's firm is compliance. It doesn't contribute directly to his firm's top line, but his firm will not grow successfully without emphasizing it. Going the opposite route, where you pursue growth at all costs, will likely lead to a disaster like Enron.

Metrics That Give You a Real Edge

So how do you identify the metrics that matter? The KPIs you choose should be as critical as the red warning light Ron once noticed flashing on his cockpit dashboard. A little more than a decade ago, he was crossing the Grand Tetons during a flight from the West Coast to Omaha. Ron knew the moment he saw the red light that the plane was experiencing generator failure. He had to land the plane with only twenty minutes of remaining battery power. He landed in Jackson Hole, Wyoming, with a scant two minutes to spare. On another, more recent flight, Ron was at an altitude of 38,000 feet when a red light signaled that he was rapidly losing cabin pressure. In just a few seconds he would lose consciousness. As a result of the plane's KPI, he was able to quickly don his oxygen mask and take the plane into a dive of 6,000 feet per minute, as he'd been trained. His laser focus on the task at hand saved his life again.

The cost of a pilot ignoring critical indicators in a plane is death. In a firm, it's business failure. To uncover the most important KPIs to monitor at your firm, look at them through the lens of your own health. Your heart has to beat for you to survive, so tracking your resting heart rate will help you keep an eye on how healthy you are. As CEO, you want to measure the equivalent—what keeps the organization healthy and will enable it to survive for the long term.

The typical core measurements that are critical to a firm's survival pertain to cash, the lifeblood of the business. In wealth management firms, like those run by Ron and Scott, they may include numbers like top-line revenue, bottom-line revenue, asset growth, and customer satisfaction. You should take note of critical numbers specific to your industry or your firm. At Cornerstone Wealth, the KPIs for which Scott holds himself personally accountable are tied to revenue growth. They include the amount of new advisory assets signed per month and the number of firms he has attracted to Carson Institutional Alliance. Other members of Scott's leadership team are responsible for different key metrics in their areas of the business.

Scott's team tracks their numbers on scorecards, with indicators of red, yellow, and green, showing if the individual is keeping the metric on track (green) or if performance in that area is slipping into the danger zone (red). As Scott tells his team, red doesn't mean you get hit over the head. It means your colleagues will help you get back on track. At his weekly meetings, all team members provide an update on how they are doing on their goals. Often, the act of verbalizing this helps them identify where they are stuck and to find ways to break through obstacles with their colleagues. Scott is not afraid or unwilling to ask for support from his team. When he set a stretch goal of bringing a large amount of new assets into the firm and found himself in the danger zone, he asked his entire team to rally around him to help achieve the goal. With everyone pitching in, the firm brought the indicator back into the green.

KPIs that help you track costs that affect your profits are also essential. Scott uses a simple scorecard to measure revenue-per-internal stakeholder. (This is a measure most firms call revenue-per-employee). Doing so helps Scott keep an eye on what the firm is spending on internal stakeholders—typically one of the biggest investments in any business. This also makes it easy for his team to see if they have achieved the goal he set for that quarter. Hitting that benchmark means his internal stakeholders receive their maximum quarterly bonuses—and going below it means they don't.

Since Scott began using this system, several key players have offered to take on new responsibilities when others have left, keeping the revenue-per-internal stakeholder figure high.

The results of tracking this single metric have been amazing. In 2010, the firm had nine internal stakeholders. Today there are six. Despite a 40 percent decrease in the number of internal stakeholders—and lower investment in labor—the recurring revenue from his firm has increased 250 percent. The members of Scott's team share all profits above revenue per internal stakeholder. As a result, they don't want him to hire an unnecessary person because that would reduce their own income. They, too, are invested in achieving the Sustainable Edge. Ron's firm has its own compensation plan that rewards internal stakeholders financially for their discretionary efforts—doing what they are capable of—rather than for doing just the bare minimum to perform the job.

It may take some experimenting to find the perfect mix of KPIs to track. When Ron first started Carson Wealth, he would spend ten hours a week monitoring data on every aspect of his firm. He is a natural planner and found it fun and interesting. But gradually, he opted for a less-is-more approach to management, simplifying what he tracked and really focusing in on the key KPIs. For each metric he monitored, he asked himself, "Does it really matter?" That helped him pare down. For instance, rather than measure random acts of kindness internal stakeholders committed on a weekly basis, he's found it more meaningful to do a "climate survey" among internal stakeholders once a year to measure the strength of the firm's culture. Now, every Friday, he reviews only the numbers that fuel sustainable growth on his "business dashboard." These numbers measure how many accounts were opened at Carson Wealth, how many assets came into the firm, how many appointments the firm had, and what the pipeline was relative to the week before. The key is to measure the aggregate picture at your firm and avoid getting caught up in tracking minutia.

Measurements that do really matter to your firm this year may fall away next year, as your team fixes problems it is working on. Don't be afraid to let them go. For instance, when Ron noticed that many meetings at Carson Wealth were starting late, he began tracking the number that started on time. But once 99 percent of the meetings began on time, he stopped recording that metric. Your metrics may even change quarterly. When Scott began planning a seminar with a business broker who works with similar clients, he set a KPI of working on it two hours a week. But when they decided not to pursue the seminar, that KPI naturally fell away, making room for another.

The IQ Grower™ process will help you choose and focus on the right KPIs. Think of them as your firm's business dashboard—just like Ron's plane has a cockpit dashboard. As you work through the IQ Grower™ process, you will set goals for the next twenty years. The indicators you incorporate into your dashboard should tell you if you are moving in the right direction to achieve your business goals. They should play a role identical to the indicators on the dashboard of Ron's plane—more often than not, indicating that you will have a safe flight, but sometimes warning you of an impending issue.

Track Leading and Lagging Indicators

To keep your firm's key metrics moving in the right direction, you'll want to monitor both leading and lagging indicators. To envision how these work, imagine you want to lose weight. Keys to your future success, like drinking a gallon of water, having a salad for lunch, or exercising for forty minutes are leading indicators of your progress toward that goal. A lagging indicator is one that follows an event or, in the case of the weight loss example, what follows your change in daily habits. So, when you step on the scale to note how much you weigh, you are looking at a lagging indicator.

Now let's look at a wealth advisory firm. Whether you are in an advisory business or manufacturing you want to determine what your leading and lagging indicators are. A leading indicator might be how many referrals you receive, while a lagging indicator is the total assets your team brought into the firm. When it comes to customer service, a leading indicator is the number of times you are "touching" a client—to let them know about the services your firm offers that could benefit them—or how much time you spend with your best clients. A lagging indicator might be the Raving Fan Index (RFI) that Ron's firm uses to measure customer satisfaction. To find examples in your industry, visit www.kpilibrary.com.

At Ron's firm, some of the KPIs he monitors on a daily are leading indicators. For instance, every day he can see how many actions his advisors have taken to follow the firm's Productivity Management System. It is designed to help them bring new assets into the firm. Another leading indicator Ron monitors is conversions

RFI Chart

On a scale of 1 to 10 (1 being low and 10 being high) please rate the following:

1. Are your phone calls to our office answered promptly and courteously by our receptionist?
   Rating: _____

   How important is this to you?
   Rating: _____

2. Are your phone calls promptly returned from our team?
   Rating: _____

   How important is this to you?
   Rating: _____

3. Are your questions answered to your satisfaction, the first time?
   Rating: _____

   How important is this to you?
   Rating: _____

4. Is the frequency of your portfolio review meetings adequate for your needs?
   Rating: _____

   How important is this to you?
   Rating: _____

5. How would you rate the overall level of SERVICE received?
   Rating: _____

   How important is this to you?
   Rating: _____

6. Our goal is to provide you with the best service experience you have ever had. Are we currently providing that?

YES _____   NO _____

If you answered NO, what do we need to do to earn a higher rating?

_____

7. Please provide us with your current email address: _____

_____

8. How satisfied are you with the management of your portfolio and overall advice from your advisor? _____

_____

9. What do you think differentiates us from other companies of any industry with which you have worked? _____

_____

10. Referrals are the primary way that we grow. Whom do you know that would benefit from receiving information about our firm?

Name _____

Phone _____

Address _____

11. If there is anyone on our team other than your advisor whom you would like to recognize for demonstrating superior service in the last year, please indicate below:

Name _____

Service Performed _____

Please do not enter any personally identifiable information (e.g., a social security number, account number, birth date, etc.) in this survey. Questions or concerns related to specific accounts should be submitted directly to your advisor.

vs. opportunities. He needs to know which advisors are telling the firm's story successfully and conveying the firm's value proposition when a prospect calls the firm. If the advisors make the most of the opportunities, there should be a 95 percent conversion rate for prospects the firm has vetted. Ron also monitors lagging indicators. For instance, his business dashboard shows assets under management for individual advisors and for the firm as a whole. When it comes to operations, for instance, Ron's dashboard shows if the company is getting cases opened or closed. That is a simple leading indicator for what service looks like.

While airplane dashboards are built from sophisticated and expensive gadgets, yours doesn't have to be. We recommend using a visual tool that can be updated easily in real time and viewed easily by all of the key players on your team. At Scott's firm, his tool of choice is a spreadsheet in Google Docs, as shown in Appendix C. Ron's firm uses a proprietary tool called the Client Experience Optimizer.

———

Building checks and balances into your metrics is important. Achieving the minimum 15 percent growth imperative is only worthwhile if you can retain your new customers through exceptional execution and excellent customer service. Your goal should be balanced growth, in which you maintain high standards as you expand. Metrics that keep your team honest about your success in this are essential. If a measure of customer satisfaction, such as Ron's RFI , is slipping, that might mean you are growing too fast. It can also point to a performance issue. One of Ron's associate business owners kept showing a poor conversion rate, despite the good opportunities the firm was putting in front of him. Ron suspected that the advisor's mind was elsewhere or there was a training issue— or both. Without the metrics to alert Ron, he might not have known to address the problem. Because he did, Ron and the poorly performing advisor came to a mutual agreement that the advisor would leave the firm. Keeping balanced growth and high standards at the forefront of his leadership, Ron builds in checks and balances to his metrics and ensures that Carson Wealth remains on track.

"Achieving the minimum 15 percent growth imperative is only worthwhile if you can retain your new customers through exceptional execution and excellent customer service."

Meeting Rhythms and Accountability

Establishing clear meeting rhythms is just as important as making sure everyone on your leadership team can easily track your KPIs. Meetings are essential to good communication, but we have found that it is important to keep the number of meetings to a minimum. At Carson Wealth, Ron's leadership team has a five-minute standing meeting every morning, one weekly meeting, and one monthly one-hour check-in. There also are quarterly and annual meetings, scheduled a year ahead of time so Ron's team can plan for them.

Scott's team follows similar rhythms. If a meeting must be added to cover a pressing topic like marketing, Scott schedules it immediately before or just after the daily 8:30 a.m. meeting to avoid breaking up the rest of the day. Interruptions can cost you and your internal stakeholders a significant amount of time and energy, because it takes so long to get back on track. The example you set for meetings as leader—both how you schedule and run your meetings—will set the tone for the rest of the team and discourage your internal stakeholders from calling too many meetings. Ron estimates that 20 percent of the firm's meetings get canceled unless they are absolutely necessary. He is constantly reviewing and evaluating how he manages his and his team's time.

Setting a clear meeting agenda is essential to prevent time wasting. Both of us open some meetings by asking our teams to share good news. While we don't allow a lot of time for small talk, we recognize that our team members may spend more time with each other than with their families and keeping them connected is important to building a strong culture. At Scott's weekly meetings, his team follows the good news by reviewing their scorecard. Including the scorecard review on your agenda makes it difficult for people, including yourself, to wiggle out of their responsibilities. Scorecard review can identify areas of your business that are slipping through the cracks. For example, one of Scott's KPIs is to make a certain

Cornerstone Weekly Meeting   *2/23/2015*

Weekly Agenda: 30–60 Minutes	
5 Min.	Good News: Everyone share two good news stories from past week, one personal, one business. Make sure everyone participates.
Debbie	
Erica	
Amy	

5–10 Min.	The Numbers: Review everyone's individual or team weekly measure of productivity.
Debbie	
Erica	
Amy	

10 Min.	Customer and Employee Data: What or where are the recurring issues or concerns that the team or its customers are facing day in and day out? Choose one issue. Assign a person or small group to explore and get to the root cause of it.
Debbie	
Erica	
Amy	

Review Previous: Who What When Accountability

Review Upcoming: Meetings and Appointments

10–30 Min.	Collective Intelligence: This should focus on a rock or a large priority. Get everyone's input and drill into one of your big issues. Make a presentation on one of your rocks with the person accountable leading it.
Choices:	
1	
2	
3	
4	

Any comments on how to improve the Morning Meeting?	
What should we start doing, stop doing, or keep doing?	
Debbie	
Erica	
Amy	

number of calls to prospects every week. When he noticed during scorecard review that he had put off those calls and slipped into the "red" zone for several weeks in a row, he recommitted to hitting that KPI by making it a top priority in his personal Essential Six and Most Vital. Scorecard review is as important to the team lead as it is to the members of the team.

When you make scorecard review a key component of your meetings, there is no place for team members to hide when they are not meeting their KPIs. One of the benefits here is, as a leader, in a one-on-one meeting, individuals can give really good stories as to why something was or was not completed or done. But in front of peers that is not so easy. At a recent weekly meeting, an internal stakeholder listed a quarterly KPI as green, which appeared acceptable to Scott. However, other stakeholders questioned it, as they knew of assets lost that same quarter, making the KPI yellow instead of green. Scott is now enjoying his best year ever by meeting his KPIs to bring in new assets critical to Cornerstone Wealth's growth.

As you know, if you watch any kind of competitive sport, keeping score is what motivates everyone to play their best—to try to achieve the next level of performance and to work toward the same goal. Without a scoreboard, everyone's efforts are unfocused. Using the right measurements in your firm will help you keep your team moving in the same direction and increase productivity exponentially. That is crucial to winning the Sustainable Edge.

IQ Grower™ Exercises to Measure What Matters

List your firm's key metrics. Are they essential? Are there any that can be removed from your list?

What is the optimal schedule for you to review them?

Should you use a KPI that measures revenue-per-internal stakeholder?

What does a more simplified system of tracking metrics look like? Can you take advantage of a third-party product or service to support your own efforts? Do you have the manpower to create your own dashboard for key stats?

Are you currently monitoring numbers that don't provide value? Are you busy without balance, tracking and reviewing metrics that are not contributing your 15 percent growth? If so, you may want to start using a scorecard like Ron and Scott to help you and your team stay focused.

What are your firm's leading and lagging indicators?

What is the rhythm of your meetings? What can you do to establish a clear rhythm for your meetings? Do you always prepare an agenda, and how can you incorporate your scorecard into it?

How can your scorecard be improved to incorporate and measure your KPIs?

Resource Link

KPIs:

http://kpilibrary.com

7.

SIMPLIFY AND LEAP FORWARD

Early in the life of Carson Wealth, Ron faced a big dilemma. He and his team had been elated when the firm won its largest account ever—one that made up 20 percent of the young company's revenue. The client had fired his previous advisors to come on board at Carson Wealth—it was a huge vote of confidence for Ron's firm. But, after about six months of working together, the client began to ask Ron and his team to do things differently than they had before and contrary to what they knew to be their best practices.

The relationship was not working out. The client didn't want to give Ron's firm discretion on the account. They wanted the team to send research reports before making each trade—at the time a very cumbersome process. What was even worse, the client was very arrogant and condescending to Ron's team when he called to check in on them every day. He was so mean and belittling that no one wanted to return his phone calls. Working this way was throwing Ron's firm into chaos. He could see that dealing with the client would eventually destroy his team's morale.

Finally, Ron made the tough but necessary decision. "I'm going to fire the client," he told the team. Everyone thought he was crazy. "You're going to fire our biggest client?" they asked. Yes," Ron told them. "In the long term, our firm will be better off."

When Ron met with the client to tell him Carson Wealth wanted to part ways with him, he was numb and afraid of what the decision would mean for the future of his firm. The client was incredulous. "You mean you're asking me to transfer my account out of the firm?" he asked. "I can hardly believe it myself, but that's exactly what I'm asking you to do," Ron responded. He recalls now that it felt like an out-of-body experience, but it was one of the best decisions he has ever made for his career. Jumping through hoops to please that client—with little to show for it—drove home how important it was to simplify his firm's focus. While accommodating every client, no matter what, once seemed like the best way to grow the firm, he realized that doing so would prevent him from delivering the niche service he so strongly believes in. He knew both he and his firm would be better off by paring down and simplifying.

Since then, Ron has really stuck by his "ideal client" paradigm and makes sure his team knows how to identify that client. The firm documented the profile of the ideal client, including important characteristics like the size of the account—at least $1 million in investable assets—and the demeanor of the account holder. For example, the ideal client is a financial delegator who appreciates feedback and is willing to follow and implement the firm's advice. With this definition in mind, the firm now says no to new clients as often as it says yes.

> *"Focusing on what is most important to your growth—instead of chasing what's interesting— will help you achieve the Sustainable Edge, too."*

Narrowing the firm's prospects might seem like it would slow the growth of Carson Wealth, but it has had just the opposite effect. The more simplified Ron's firm has become, the faster it has grown and the more sustainable its edge. Focusing on what is most important to your growth—instead of chasing what's interesting—will help you achieve the Sustainable Edge, too.

Monitor Productivity

We've already discussed the importance of setting goals and priorities for yourself and your business. Each day, you and your team must make many decisions about how you use your time in order to achieve your shared goals. In the interest of simplifying, that means radically reducing the demands on your time and attention.

Ron created a Productivity Management System to serve just that purpose for his team. The system is built off of Steven Covey's four quadrant system of time management. Each team member divides

Productivity Management System:
4 Quadrants

Important/ Urgent	Important/ Not Urgent
Not Important/ Urgent	Harmful/ Wasteful

the day's tasks into four quadrants—important and urgent (upper left quadrant), important but not urgent (upper right quadrant), unimportant and not urgent (bottom right quadrant), and wasteful (lower left quadrant). Ideally, 90 percent of the day should be spent on tasks that are important and urgent, or important and nonurgent, and only 10 percent of your time should be spent on tasks that are unimportant. If you can't complete what is important and urgent or important and nonurgent during your typical workday, consider coming into work sixty to ninety minutes earlier than your team to give yourself the critical "think time" you need. Scott has learned that he is most productive when he devotes ninety minutes of focused time first thing in the morning to the most important priority on his Essential Six.

To build off of and enhance the four quadrant system, Ron established a point system for his internal stakeholders. They earn points based on how many important and urgent and important and nonurgent tasks they accomplish, such as serving an A-plus client, passion prospecting, or working out. They don't get points if they work on something that is unimportant. As the team lead, Ron has found there is a direct correlation between high points and high results. The Productivity Management System works especially well in conjunction with the Essential Six, with each system reinforcing the other. Because of the synergy between the two systems, Ron even prioritizes working on the Essential Six as an important daily task for his team members.

Productivity Management System

Week of: _____

Points	15	15	15	12	10	10
Activity	Wealth Plan Presentation to "A+" Prospect	"A+" Prospect Meeting	Passion Event for "A+" Client and/or Prospect	Plan Next Week in Detail (Max 12 Points / Week)	Develop Centers of Influence	Work Out 1 Hour / Day
Monday						
Tuesday						
Wednesday						
Thursday						
Friday						
Saturday						
Sunday						
Weekly Total	0	0	0	0	0	0

Points	5	5	5	5	5	4
Activity	Prepare for Next Day (Plan the Night Before for 1 Hour Max)	Dry Run of Wealth Plan	Creative Thinking and/or Planning (Max 1 Hour / Week)	Annual Review with "A" Client	Staff Development (Every ½ Hour)	Any "A+" or "A" Client and/or Prospect Interaction (5 Minutes Minimum)
Monday						
Tuesday						
Wednesday						
Thursday						
Friday						
Saturday						
Sunday						
Weekly Total	0	0	0	0	0	0

Directions—Each workday, either throughout the day or at the end of the day, enter the number of points for each of the tasks completed. If you received two referrals from A+ clients, give yourself 20 points in the corresponding column and row. Then, aim to increase your score each week.

10	7	6	6	5	5	5	5
Receive a Referral from "A+" Client	Annual Review with "A+" Client	Wealth Plan Presentation to "A" Prospect	"A" Prospect Meeting	Wealth Plan Demo	Meal with "A+" Client or Prospect (or Equivalent)	Receive a Referral from "A" Client	Passion Event for "A" Client
0	0	0	0	0	0	0	0

(continued below)

4	4	4	3	3	3	2	
Implement Peak Advisor Alliance Material (4 Points / ½ Hour– Max 2 Hours / Week)	Account Aggregation for Client	Coaching Session with Peak Advisor Alliance	Professional Development (3 Points / ½ Hour– Max 2 Hours / Week)	Handling "A+" Client Issues (Every ½ Hour)	Review Goal Cards and Record Notes	Peer Networking	**Daily Total**
0	0	0	0	0	0	0	0

Productivity Management System (continued)

Essential Six

MOST VITAL: _____
(Activity that must be accomplished this week, in business or personal life)

MONDAY

1. _____
2. _____
3. _____
4. _____
5. _____
6. _____

TUESDAY

1. _____
2. _____
3. _____
4. _____
5. _____
6. _____

WEDNESDAY

1. _____
2. _____
3. _____
4. _____
5. _____
6. _____

THURSDAY

1. _____
2. _____
3. _____
4. _____
5. _____
6. _____

FRIDAY

1. _____
2. _____
3. _____
4. _____
5. _____
6. _____

SATURDAY

1. _____
2. _____
3. _____
4. _____
5. _____
6. _____

SUNDAY

1. _____
2. _____
3. _____
4. _____
5. _____
6. _____

THINGS TO DO

1. _____
2. _____
3. _____
4. _____
5. _____
6. _____

MORE THINGS TO DO

7. _____
8. _____
9. _____
10. _____
11. _____
12. _____

MISSION: _____

_____

"Like cleaning off your desk at night before you go home, the Productivity Management System clears the clutter in your mind."

Like cleaning off your desk at night before you go home, the Productivity Management System clears the clutter in your mind. Beginning the day with a clean slate unleashes tremendous productivity. Remember, an essential part of achieving the Sustainable Edge is tapping in to your subconscious. Using a tool like the Productivity Management System can help you do just that. The Productivity Management System can also help you spot patterns in your productivity and plan your year accordingly. For instance, because winters in Omaha are harsh, Ron's team spends a lot of the season hunkered down at their desks working. Because of this, Ron likes to allow them to have a little more flexibility and free time in the summer. To avoid slipping behind, they will typically set a simple goal of maintaining a certain level of work during the summer. By setting themselves up for success by using a system that supports a big picture vision, Ron's team can achieve the work-life balance that is essential to achieving the Sustainable Edge.

Streamline Your Processes

Systems and processes that make your business run more efficiently are an essential component of your success. But, be careful not to load up your firm with every system that claims to improve your workflow—too many systems become inefficient and may end up using more time than saving. Just as tracking too many metrics can waste time, so can loading up your business with novel productivity-enhancing tools. Distinguish between those that are effective tools and those that aren't.

When Ron considers adding a new tool or procedure to his business, he returns to his experience as a pilot and envisions the cockpit of an airplane. There are three levels of lights that show up. White lights are informational indicators. Yellow lights indicate caution, and while they aren't immediately critical, they can become critical. Red lights convey the need for immediate attention and action from the pilot. If you add only those tools and procedures that are as critical as red lights, you will trim a lot of unnecessary clutter from of your business. The fewer indicators you monitor, the better off you are.

It is also important to reevaluate the functionality of your existing tools and procedures regularly, so you aren't wasting time on systems that no longer serve the firm. When Scott closes his team's weekly meetings every Monday morning by asking his internal stakeholders what Cornerstone Wealth should start, stop, and keep doing, he is especially curious about what they should stop doing. The team also discusses what Scott calls Hassle Logs. This is where team members list the bottlenecks they are hearing about from clients or are personally facing on a weekly basis. If they have a recurring situation wherein they find themselves asking, "Why am I doing this?" or saying, "This is taking way longer than it should," Scott urges his team to record it in the Hassle Log he keeps in Google Docs. That way, they can discuss it as a team and eliminate the time drains together.

Take a Minimal Approach to Technology

Technology can be a great time saver, but you must vet it very carefully. Make sure your business isn't derailed by systems that don't work for you—or don't work at all. You will know you are handling your technology needs effectively when you have the freedom to enjoy activities away from the office. Sounds counter-intuitive, right? But it's not. Take Scott's recent hunting trip. When he returned to the office after spending days away from his computer, he found that everything was in order, thanks to the smooth integration of the systems in place at Cornerstone Wealth, like the Client Experience Optimizer and Microsoft Outlook. Without those tools, Scott would have spent the entire day—if not more—after vacation catching up. Ron had a similar experience recently at his hunting lodge. The Client Experience Optimizer allowed him to prepare for a Monday-morning client meeting from the lodge in only thirty minutes. That same prep work used to take an entire Sunday at the office.

So how do you make the right decisions on technology? Rather than devoting much of his own time to researching new software, Ron relies on his chief technology officer to make the right decision on whether to handle a task in-house or outsource it. Carson Wealth is a large enough firm that it is important to have someone dedicated to its technological needs. Before Ron considers adding new software, he first considers an outsourced solution. If Ron and his chief technology officer decide that their team can't create something better than an outsourced provider, they gladly outsource. Human capital is the most sacred resource at his firm, so Ron guards the capacity of his internal stakeholders very carefully.

This has not happened by chance. Ron's team has invested considerable time and money to come up with a well-coordinated technology game plan. Using one-off technologies that do not "talk" to each other will prevent your firm from scaling up effectively. With each decision on new technology, Ron and his entire team ask, "Can this technology support our ultimate goal to become a $50 billion or $100 billion firm?" It is about making decisions not just for where they are but also for where they want to go. Ron always acts on his immediate goals with his Most Vital at the forefront of his actions. Carson Wealth also invests heavily in training to make sure its team uses technology in the most effective way. Otherwise, much of the firm's investment will be lost as team members scramble to get up to speed with new programs. In Scott's firm, where he does not need as large a tech staff, he and his team ask themselves a simple question before adding new technology, "Will it make our lives easier or create more clutter to learn this?"

At the same time, it is important not to over-rely on technology. Some internal stakeholders may have a tendency to "hide" by entering information about meeting key goals into systems and spreadsheets they know you don't check frequently. Printing out Google

Docs or other records you use to monitor your company's performance will make them more visible to you. It's also important to make sure your team actually provides quality information no matter what technology you use. Making decisions based on incomplete information will put your firm at risk.

Clearing Clutter

As a leader, you may find you get "constipated" with stuff piling up in your mind. You need a way to relieve the "gas" in your head. This may sound wacky, but Ron uses the FARTS (File, Act on it, Respond to it, Trash, or Suspend) system to keep track of ideas. Materials can be filed when they no longer require attention; filing gets them out of sight. Acting on an idea entails doing something concrete about it. Responding means getting back to someone. Trashing it means if it's not needed, don't keep it around. Finally, suspending it means taking it as far as he can until someone else gets him information on it. As a result of using this approach, Ron has streamlined his work and minimized the amount of clutter on his desks at the office and at home. It is a great way to eliminate excess baggage from his professional life and keep his mind clear.

> *"To free space for what is truly important to you, like family and exercise are for each of us, you have to say no to distractions."*

Once you have become crystal clear on your goals through the IQ Grower™ exercises, you will have to make tough decisions on what to get rid of, so you can focus on what is most important. As an entrepreneur, it is easy to fill your time up with activities that sound amazing, especially when you have the funds to afford them. To free space for what is truly important to you, like family and exercise are for each of us, you have to say no to distractions.

Our point of view is that you must be a little selfish to be selfless. Put off your own needs and priorities too much and you will not be able to help anyone else who relies on you. By being a little selfish in the short term, you can be more selfless in the long term.

When you run a business where you are visible in your community, it is easy to take on social obligations that devour time better spent on deep relationships or that would be more wisely devoted to taking care of your own health and well-being. We have both struggled at times to simplify our lives in this way. Ron and his family used to have an over-committed social life, but now he has learned when to say no. Not long ago, friends asked him and Jeanie to host an event at their club. He bowed out by telling his friends that he and Jeanie were too busy to enjoy hosting, so they couldn't accept. What a thoughtful and polite way to honor your boundaries without being rude. Of course, saying no to invitations like this won't please everyone in your circle. But if you say yes when you can't afford the time, it is likely you'll end up pleasing no one. Say yes to everything, and you won't be happy, your family won't be happy, and you will stretch yourself so thin that even those to whom you are giving time will not be pleased. The people who have the deepest relationships with you will understand when you say you can't make something work.

Being really clear on your personal goals from the IQ Grower™ process can help you make tough decisions in this regard. One of Scott's goals for 2014 was to focus on his wife, Angie, their two children, and his parents. He is one of five children, which makes it very difficult to attend all family events. Around the holidays it is especially challenging to make everyone happy, given that he and Angie also want to spend time with her family. This year, he had to say no to certain activities, so he could prioritize his immediate family and his parents. That upset a couple of his siblings, but he realized he simply could not be everywhere all of the time. By staying focused on the key relationships he identified as most important to him in the moment, he was able to maintain his commitment to meeting his father for breakfast every Friday. Memories of their breakfasts are irreplaceable and comforting to Scott now that his father has passed.

Living simply isn't a simple task. But if you want to achieve what is most meaningful to you, it is important to make the tough decisions that will allow you to lead a richer, more rewarding, and meaningful life. That is what the Sustainable Edge is all about.

IQ Grower™ Exercises to Simplify and Leap Forward

What demands are monopolizing your time and attention at home and at work? How can you streamline these demands, so you are focusing on your top priorities in both life areas?

Does your technology work for or against you? If it's working against you, what steps can you take to turn things around?

Would you benefit from a Productivity Management System? How would you incorporate it into your firm's processes? How would it work, and can you envision any roadblocks from your staff in its implementation and use? If so, what steps could you take to make the transition to this new system smoother?

Are you sufficiently protecting and managing your human capital by tasking team members to execute on appropriate goals? Have you taken on tasks that should remain on their desks? Do you need to reassess the division of labor within your organization or put in place a dedicated expert (such as Ron's chief technology officer)?

Have you been selfless to your own detriment? How can you be more selfish in order to benefit the greater good?

Resource Link

TED Talk:

http://www.ted.com/talks/graham_hill_less_stuff_more_happiness

8.

BE BOLDLY VULNERABLE AND
RECEIVE THE BEST IN RETURN

On a ride from the hunting lodge to Ron's office, Ron recently asked Robert Moore, former president of LPL Financial and current CEO of Legal & General Investment Management America, what one thing has led to his success. "It's being vulnerable," Moore told him. "When you're a leader, if you go into an organization and people think you think you've got all the answers, they want to prove you wrong. If instead you say, 'You know, I don't know' and ask for their help with sincerity, you will demonstrate a strong leadership quality that most leaders really lack," he explained. By being honest about what he doesn't know and turning to his team for answers, Moore has accelerated his company's success. Moore allows himself to be "boldly vulnerable." (We came up with "boldly vulnerable," because we felt that "vulnerable" simply didn't capture the power of Moore's intention well enough.) He isn't afraid to be transparent and candid, even at the risk of public exposure for being wrong or for not knowing how to solve a problem. That takes courage and humility.

> "When you're a leader, if you go into an organization and people think you think you've got all the answers, they want to prove you wrong."

Many leaders start out by taking the exact opposite approach. Ron, in fact, had more of a "Do it my way or the highway" style early in his career. He thought that admitting he didn't have an answer made him look weak. He wasn't afraid to invite his team to challenge him. But when someone had an idea that was different from his own, he would belittle it and, in doing so, belittle the team member. He eventually realized that he was squashing every ounce of imagination and creativity from his team and creating an unhealthy and unproductive working environment. It was a lonely place for him, and it was not furthering his goals for the firm.

Over time, Ron allowed himself to be more vulnerable and open, which helped him create a very collaborative, collegial environment where he feels like more of a partner with his team. Now he has lunch every quarter with all of the new members of the firm. When dining with seven new internal stakeholders recently, they told him how refreshing it was to know their ideas were being heard in the supportive and protective environment the firm has created. "My goal is to send you home happy every day," Ron told them, and he sincerely meant it. Hearing that they do go home happy— and know they are a critical part of the value the firm brings to its clients—underscores what a transformation he has made in his leadership skills.

Today, Ron has reached a point where he loves saying, "I don't know." He considers himself a librarian, not a library. Instead of feeling like he has to know everything—or look like he does—he surrounds himself with smart people and the right resources. By showing he is human, admitting his mistakes, and demonstrating through real action that he sincerely cares about others, he has greatly improved his effectiveness as a leader. In order to make sure he and other executives at the firm receive continuous feedback on how they are performing in this regard, Carson Wealth has used and now uses Gallops Q12360-degree reviews where anyone can offer anonymous comments.

Scott embraces his vulnerability as a leader in a different way at Cornerstone Wealth. When his firm held an offsite retreat in 2009, his team members did an exercise where they went around the room and suggested two things each person does well and two things they need to work on. Scott knew this would leave everyone feeling a bit exposed, so he asked the team to give him feedback first. His team told him he starts a lot of things he doesn't finish. He wasn't surprised. His natural tendency to embrace risk has been both a blessing and a liability throughout his life. But the feedback from his team made him realize he needed to recalibrate his natural tendency and ask for more support on executing projects.

Trust Starts with You

Today, leaders and their teams must be boldly vulnerable—they must be ready to give and receive the truth. Otherwise, you leave your firm open to damaging situations like the one facing General Motors in 2014. GM was facing a multistate investigation and a major lawsuit by the state of Arizona for its handling of a deadly ignition-switch defect that critics said should have been disclosed to the public years earlier. In a smaller firm, a single situation like this will put you out of business.

So how do you create a culture of communication that is above-board, honest, and direct? You must embody those values as a leader and cultivate your listening skills. Otherwise, it will be easy for you to get blindsided by competitors who may not have even existed last year, new technologies changing the landscape of your industry, or a problem that's brewing in your own firm. No team member will want to speak up when they spot trouble—whether it comes from outside the firm or within—if they know you're likely to "kill the messenger." Many leaders think they have done all they can on this front because they are honest people who are not trying to hide anything or deceive anyone. But that still leaves room for improvement. Often, even the best leaders realize there is room to make big strides in communication that will power their firm's growth.

"No team member will want to speak up when they spot trouble—whether it comes from outside the firm or within—if they know you're likely to "kill the messenger.""

Years ago, Scott found his team rolling their eyes when he started a meeting by saying how important it was to live the firm's six core values: passion, hard work and determination, innovation, first class, down to earth, and ownership mindset. It wasn't the first time he'd emphasized this message and he could see his team thinking, "Here we go again." Then it dawned on him that there was a better way to inspire his internal stakeholders—improving his own listening skills. Like many "Type A" entrepreneurs, Scott is so action oriented that he has a tendency to bulldoze conflict. He had to improve on his truth receiving and his truth giving in order to get his team to be more open with him.

In a meeting with his mentor, Scott decided to take a different approach to truthfulness—one that took cold vulnerability. He apologized to his team for how he'd handled conflict in the past and promised to make a conscious effort to listen better. After owning that he had contributed to conflict and distrust, he found that his internal stakeholders were more comfortable challenging him in face-to-face meetings. Scott knew he had succeeded when several key players shared they thought service was slipping. After a forty-five-minute discussion, they came to an agreement about the direction the firm should take. It was Scott who made the final call, but only after everyone else had been heard. By demonstrating that he is a good truth receiver, Scott freed his team members to be good truth givers when the stake are high.

To keep the lines of communication open, Scott often reminds his team that he isn't invested in who is right and wrong. They are all there to serve the firm's clients and find the best ways to do so. That has made an important difference in the quality of the conversations the firm has had. Today, the firm's culture has evolved so much that Scott starts its quarterly meetings by calling out two team members whose actions embody the firm's core values. He has so many stories to share that it's hard to choose just two. That's where your firm needs to be if you want to keep the Sustainable Edge.

Take a Scientific Approach

Making observations, instead of jumping to immediate conclusions, can go a long way toward building a culture of openness and trust. Sheldon Harris, who has advised Ron's firm as a business coach and consultant, was president of Cold Stone Creamery for close to a decade. As a young warehouse manager at his previous company, Costco, Harris noticed a new team member named Cody was regularly arriving late to work. Irate about it, Harris began documenting Cody's tardiness, so he could issue a formal written warning. After the third lateness he marched into Cody's office and, with a "gotcha" tone in his voice said, "You're late!"

"Do you want to know why?" Cody asked. He continued, "On my first three days working here I observed that you tend to park your car clear across the parking lot. When you walk in for your shift, you clear all the trash and the loose carts that are banging into people's cars—you're working before you even walk into the building. I figured if it was good enough for my manager to do, then it's good enough for me. So now I do that every day. Some days it takes a little longer, so I get into the building a little later."

"Making observations, instead of jumping to immediate conclusions, can go a long way toward building a culture of openness and trust."

It was a humbling moment for Harris. He had pounced on someone he should have been trying to clone. Imagine how differently the situation would have gone if Harris had said, "Cody, I noticed you were late today. Is everything okay?" Now Harris teaches the executives he coaches how to shift to an observer's mindset to encourage open communication. Working on your own leadership skills in this way will pay off immensely and there are many daily opportunities to do so. Scott remembers when he noticed a member of his team arriving late to several daily huddles, he immediately started to question this individual's cultural fit at the firm. One day, this individual arrived just as everyone was ready to go back to their desks. "We're shutting the meeting down," Scott said, hoping to make a point. "I'm sorry," the team member said. "I was on the phone with my doctor getting some news, and I couldn't hang up." Scott felt like he was an inch tall. Now he pushes himself to ask questions before he rushes to judgment.

One shortcut we've found to being a better truth giver and receiver is to build in meditation time into your routine. Don't worry, we're not suggesting you build a shrine and take up chanting (unless, of course, that appeals to you). Scott dedicates five minutes each morning to quiet reflection. Meditative activities, such as hiking, can play the same role. When Ron is scaling mountain peaks or practicing yoga, he becomes better able to quiet the noise and observe what is going on without overreacting to it.

Keep Your Culture Healthy

Ray Dalio, who manages about $150 billion in investments at the hedge fund Bridgewater, is so committed to creating an open, honest culture that every meeting at the firm in Greenwich, Connecticut, is recorded on video—even the team's performance reviews. This brutal transparency shapes every aspect of the firm. "In order to be excellent we need to know what's true, especially those things that we would rather not be true, so that we can decide how best to deal with them," the firm explains on its website. "We want logic and reason to be the basis for making decisions. It is through this striving to be excellent by being radically truthful and transparent that we build meaningful work and meaningful relationships."

"We want logic and reason to be the basis for making decisions. It is through this striving to be excellent by being radically truthful and transparent that we build meaningful work and meaningful relationships."

Dalio's use of video may not appeal to every firm, but to be boldly vulnerable enough to achieve the Sustainable Edge, you must find your own way to be radically transparent. There have never been more opportunities to grow exponentially than today, thanks to the technologies we've discussed in earlier chapters. But with its advances, the digital era has also brought new responsibilities. Your internal stakeholders, customers, and other stakeholders expect you to keep them informed in a way that earlier generations didn't. A Wizard of Oz approach to running a business will no longer work. You must pull back the curtain and hold it open in order to build and maintain trust and communication with your key stakeholders or your growth will not be sustainable.

Keeping your firm free of destructive politics is crucial to building and maintaining a culture of trust. We both insist that when members have problems with colleagues they discuss the issues one-on-one, not with others behind closed doors. It takes discipline and commitment to stick with your guns on this. Because most people are conflict averse, you'll find that many of your internal stakeholders would rather do anything than discuss issues or concerns openly. Some of your team members may have even developed bad habits in their previous places of employment where there was a culture of intrigue and political infighting.

Discipline on this front will pay off. At one point, Ron met with two internal stakeholders who approached him with complaints about a peer. Ron was not comfortable discussing issues without the colleague in the room and told them so. His personal litmus test on discussions about any of his internal stakeholders, "Would I say what I'm about to say with no hesitation if I knew they were listening in on the conversation?" When the two stakeholders mentioned their colleague again, Ron insisted that they stop the conversation, because he knew it was better for all to have a constructive discussion where he could offer help and support. As a result, he and all three of the internal stakeholders met a few days later and came up with a plan to resolve the issue.

Was the meeting uncomfortable? Yes. Conflict can be painful. But holding that meeting helped Ron preserve the trust among his team. You can make sure meetings like this go more smoothly if the information you share comes from a position of "We care about you," and if you assume anyone being complained about is genuinely trying to do the best they can and is fully committed to the mission. Your feedback must come from a position of support and compassion. If you discover that the person is not committed to the firm's mission, the conversation must become "Let's figure out a positive transition for you out of the firm."

Sometimes, you may have to part ways with team members whose behavior undermines trust in the organization, before it becomes a cancer. Ron had a situation like this in his firm recently. After noticing one of his key executives was habitually bulldozing his team, failing to listen to colleagues' feedback, and making excuses for every shortcoming, Ron let him go. He was surprised at what a big lift the executive's absence brought to the rest of the team.

Attract Team Members You Can Trust

Of course, recruiting people who embody trust and transparency in the first place will make your job easier. At Cold Stone Creamery, Sheldon Harris relied on a workforce made up mostly of teenagers to scoop the chain's gourmet ice cream. To attract new hires with the right personality and maturity to keep customers happy, managers would typically invite ten applicants to come to the store at one time for an unusual employment test.

"Who'd like to bust a move first?" the manager would ask. At first, everyone would sit in silence, looking around the room with uncertainty. Then a brave soul would volunteer to go first. That first person would usually offer a really good dance move—but not get called back for a second interview. They'd often return and ask, "My move was clearly the best. Why didn't you hire me?" "That wasn't the move we were watching," a manager would tell them. "We were watching what you were doing when you were outside of the circle and someone else was in the middle. Were you looking down your nose and judging them with that look on your face like I'm better than you? Or were you silently encouraging them and cheering them on to do their best, even though you could see they were struggling?"

Harris was seeking new hires with integrity in communication. He wanted to attract team members who'd be honest and straight with their colleagues, not inclined to stab them in the back when they thought no one was watching. He understood that if team members don't feel safe around each other, the Cold Stone Creamery culture would not withstand the inevitable challenges that arise when scaling a business. Harris's approach helped him build the franchise chain to one of the fastest growing in the nation—with more than 1,400 stores—by the time he left in 2006. He now coaches other companies on how to develop their own methods to screen for team members who embrace what he calls "integrity in communication."

We each have developed our own systems to screen potential hires who will embrace the honesty in communication we prize. When Ron interviews candidates at Carson Wealth, one of his favorite interview questions is, "Tell me about the last time you were dishonest. What did you do?" About a third of the people will say, "I am never dishonest." Then he'll say, "Well, tell me about a time you broke the rules. How did you break the rules?" If they say, "I never break the rules," he doesn't believe them. We're all human. There are times when we all are dishonest to some degree or break the rules. Ron will also dig into how candidates handle conflict by asking, "Tell me about a work situation that bugged you and what did you do about it?" Or, he may ask them what their weaknesses are. If they turn a weakness into a strength, he considers that a red flag. He'd much rather someone own up to the fact that there are some things they can't do well.

Ron can be brutal if he senses someone is not telling the truth. When he interviewed one advisor who said he'd planned for clients with very high net worth, Ron asked, "Tell me the most creative idea you brought to them." He was met with silence. Unrelenting, Ron followed up by asking, "Do you know what an 831(b) is?" (He was referring to an option that can help high-net-worth individuals who operate small businesses save on taxes through a captive insurance program.) When the candidate answered, "Yes," Ron countered with, "Tell me what it is." It soon became clear the candidate was bluffing. He looks for opportunities to uncover candidates who not being honest, forthright, and vulnerable, because those are the types of people who will not fit into his organization culturally. Ron wants to work shoulder-to-shoulder every day with people who lay it on the line.

Be very careful about whom you add to the mix. Building a passionate workplace culture is a little like trying to make a world-class cookie. If you add chili pepper to the ingredient list for the cookies, you won't like the results. But if you're making chili, it makes sense to add the peppers. Anyone who comes into Ron's office sees a sign that says, "Work hard. Play hard. Make a difference." He looks for people who naturally live that way. Many of the firm's recruits are happy, positive, and high-energy people who love the difference they are making in others' lives.

Every owner makes occasional mistakes in hiring. To maintain a culture of passion, Ron does not tolerate internal stakeholders who have become cancerous to the environment. His team appreciates how concerned and committed he is to keeping the environment healthy. When he occasionally parts ways with team members who don't fit the firm's culture, he has been surprised at how many of their colleagues remarked about how much better their work experience has become.

As Scott likes to put it, "Dig, dig, dig," when you are interviewing, in order to uncover specific answers to any questions you have about a candidate's integrity. Honest candidates will be happy to share their stories in great detail and to connect you to past employers who will back up what they say. If someone can't think of any anecdotes to address your questions in this area, keep pressing them for specifics and pay close attention if they balk or seem to wilt when you ask, "Can you explain that a little further?" It's important to also ask for stories from their work life and their personal life, which to us are components of a whole, living life. To build a culture that values being boldly vulnerable and embracing transparency, you must attract team members who embrace it, too, in every area of their life. It takes some time to find people like this but when you do, it will make all the difference in giving your firm the Sustainable Edge.

IQ Grower™ Exercises to Be Boldly Vulnerable and Receive the Best in Return

Are you boldly vulnerable? Recall an example of a time you were boldly vulnerable. Have you behaved in a way that resulted in unintentionally discouraged truth-giving?

Can you recall a time when you jumped to conclusions about a team member? How did it turn out, and how did it impact morale on your team? How could you handle a similar situation with bold vulnerability in the future?

Does your firm have ways of encouraging and rewarding honest feedback?

Consider your interview process and what is important for you. Can you formulate several questions or interview practices that will help you identify the best addition to your teams?

Resource Link

Meditation/Mindfulness:

www.relaxationresponse.org/steps

9.

DELIVER VALUE BEYOND A DOUBT

While in Monaco recently, Ron called the hotel concierge to book a car. The concierge told him the ride would cost the equivalent of about $300. What the concierge neglected to tell him was that the fee was not per ride but per hour. A three-hour car ride ended up costing Ron about $900. Had he found a cab outside of the hotel on his own, it would have most certainly cost a lot less. Although Ron could afford the fare, the ride was not worth $900 to him. He knew he had been taken advantage of, and it left him with a negative opinion about the hotel.

Many in Ron's generation grew up in small communities like the Nebraska farming town where Ron was raised. No one worried or thought twice about trusting businesses in the community.

Everyone knew everyone, and word traveled quickly if a business-man was dishonest or didn't deliver the value customers expected. Unfortunately, society has changed since then. We now live in a time where, if you don't ask the right questions, you'll often be taken advantage of. Many people and businesses now embrace the "every man for himself" approach. Maybe they are not technically lying to you, but they're not telling you the whole truth. This new business environment shapes how your customers and prospects view your business. Their bias is now toward distrust.

"To grow your business at a minimum of 15 percent a year and achieve the Sustainable Edge you must earn the trust of every customer and prospect."

To grow your business at a minimum of 15 percent a year and achieve the Sustainable Edge, you must earn the trust of every cus-tomer and prospect. Being boldly vulnerable and radically trans-parent, as we discussed in the last chapter, will help you achieve that goal, but there's more to the equation. To counter the distrust, you must deliver value beyond a doubt. Even if customers trust you, they won't keep coming back if you don't provide something that truly benefits them. You need to back up what you say with what you do. The value you bring must transcend the fine print of your contracts. As John Bogle said in his book, *Enough*, delivering value to your clients is about being an eighteenth-century man in a twenty-first-century society. It is about serving—not being self-serving. You've got to deliver something customers want or need, and you have to do it better than your competitors.

Many business owners feel exhausted just thinking about this. We're not surprised. When you run a small operation, it is not easy to deliver great value at a competitive price. You just don't have the resources big competitors do. And, in the global economy, you may be facing rivals who have set up shop in developing countries where overhead is lower and who are using technology to penetrate your market. These pressures are why so many small business owners are selling their firms or closing their doors. They are tired of feeling like they are isolated on an island in the middle of the ocean without a life raft.

The good news is that delivering value beyond a doubt is easier than you may think. The methods you have learned to build your Sustainable Edge will help make you a stronger competitor and allow you to enjoy the freedom and autonomy that comes with running your firm for as long as you want—no matter what competition arises.

Know What Your Customers Value

The first step to delivering value beyond a doubt is figuring out what your customers actually value—not what you think they value. They can tell you what they want better than anyone else. Asking them directly is the easiest way. Scott's firm calls clients regularly to ask how they would rate the firm and how likely they are to recommend Cornerstone Wealth to competitors. If your clients are not referring clients to you, there is likely a flaw in your service offering or how you are delivering it. When asking for client feedback, probe to find out what service offerings your competitors are offering to them. Which ones would they like you to add and why? They are constantly getting solicitations from your competitors and may know better than you what innovative new offerings are available to them.

Client advisory councils are another easy way to get direct feedback. These are groups of your ideal clients whom you ask for ideas on how to improve your services on a regular basis. Some firms hold their advisory council meetings in person, but you can also meet via conference call or videoconference. Client advisory councils may include all of your ideal clients or a subset market you would like to grow, like the councils of women and millennials Ron is currently building. The key is to schedule client advisory council meetings regularly and to plan for them intentionally. That way you can pick up on signals from the market early, when you can still get in front of trends.

You will sometimes be floored by what you learn from your advisory councils. For years, Scott's firm went to great lengths to stand out through customer intimacy, whether by sending thoughtful gifts to clients or remembering their birthdays with phone calls. But after talking with the ideal clients on his firm's advisory council, Scott realized he needed to adjust his actions. Cornerstone Wealth's clients are mostly business owners who are very bottom-line oriented. While they appreciated the personal touches the firm gave, what really made them stick with the firm and recommend it to others was one thing—results. One client drove this home especially well when Scott asked him what he would like the firm to start doing differently. The client said he wanted a simple sheet showing how his portfolio had progressed from the time he started with the firm to the present. That made Scott realize how urgent it was to improve the firm's reporting tools. By joining Carson Institutional Alliance and gaining access to its Client Experience Optimizer, Scott began to use a reporting tool—and provide the important reports to his clients—his boutique firm never could have developed on its own.

> *"The first step to delivering value beyond a doubt is figuring out what your customers actually value—not what you think they value."*

Often, if you're willing to listen, clients will give you valuable clues in off-the-cuff conversations, too. One of Ron's clients, Doug, has been with him for twenty-five years. He once said to Ron, "We love you. But our kids aren't going to work with you." Ron was floored. He had known Doug's kids since they were little. "They say you guys are just out of touch," Doug continued. As he explained to Ron, they were already using online accounts where they could get instant access to crucial information. Doug's comments—and similar ones from valued clients—lit a fire under Ron and his other stakeholders. They had to make sure the firm evolved, so it could stay relevant.

When you get feedback like this, it is easy to fall into the trap of defending what you are comfortable with instead of embracing the unknown. Ron and his advisors initially dismissed the online offerings their clients told them about, thinking these would never replace the human touch their firm provided. But when they went online and looked at the sophisticated reporting tools other firms were offering, they realized their clients were spot on. Ron changed his opinion and concluded the future belongs to firms that deliver maximum technology and meaningful touch. Remember the Lee Majors character in the 1970s TV series *The Six Million Dollar Man*? As Ron now sees it, the future is in the "bionic" advisory experience, combining the best of man and machine. Forcing yourself to be realistic about what is happening in your industry may be painful. It was for Ron. But facing facts will help you make new trends in your industry work in your favor, so you can gain the Sustainable Edge.

Change Your Mindset About Profit

Some of the things your clients want, like new technology, may be expensive to provide. So how do you do that and still maintain high profits? Perhaps you can't. You may be surprised to hear this from us—we're both enthusiastic capitalists—but to deliver value beyond a doubt, you must rethink the idea of profit. Achieving too high a margin is not healthy for your business.

In the late 1990s, margins at Ron's firm were much higher than today. But as the firm grew, he had an epiphany. Having a high-margin advisory business isn't one and the same as delivering the best service. Sharing the wealth with both internal stakeholders and the firm's clients, he realized, was the best thing he could do to achieve the Sustainable Edge for the long term. That meant compensating his team very well and providing the highest-value service to his clients. If he kept pursuing the highest possible margins, he realized, he would lose the talent, customers, and purpose he needed for his business to thrive in the long-term. He would regret spending his life building a firm that provided less than it could to our clients. Ultimately, he would hurt the value of everything he was building.

Don't get us wrong. We're not advocating socialism here. To achieve the Sustainable Edge, you must maintain a responsible profit margin. Find out what the average margin is in your industry and set a goal to double that. You need to be able to invest in and retain great people and create enough of a margin of safety that you can stay in business. By sharing profits with the internal stakeholders who act like owners, you will ultimately help the firm grow.

To deliver value beyond a doubt, you need the right people. These are professionals who see their work as a calling—not just a job to make money or even a career. They are serving a higher purpose. These people are rare, and you will have to pay them more. That will reduce your profit margins. At the same time, these folks will typically do the work of three people and elevate your firm and its service offerings in ways you might not have imagined possible. Even if paying them higher salaries reduces your profits, these valuable team members are crucial to achieving the Sustainable Edge. Having them on your team will always trump the most ruthless bottom-line focus in the long run.

Team Up to Accomplish More

Ron recently spent a weekend with a business owner at his hunting lodge. The owner talked about how he handles the growing complexity of his industry. He spends one day of every week on compliance and one day a week on research. Ron was incredulous. "You're kidding yourself," Ron wanted to say. "There's no way you can keep up with compliance in one day a week. There's no way you can do research in one day a week and truly service a client." The advisor's approach is like trying to be an NFL coach by coaching one day a week. We all know that coaching is a seven-day-a-week job. A coach who attempts to do the job in one day is cheating the team and his fans. The same holds true in the wealth management industry. Compliance is a full-time job. Research is a full-time job. You can't just commit one day a week to each of these things and deliver a niche service to your clients.

Part of delivering value in a small business is recognizing when you can't do certain things at the highest level on your own. Attempting to perform critical tasks that require specialized expertise that you don't have is like performing open-heart surgery when you haven't gone to medical school. Ask yourself some tough questions about your skills and be honest about the answers. Knowing what you know about your own capabilities, would you hire your firm to perform all of the tasks you are doing for your clients? Can you grow at a minimum of 15 percent a year and compete with anyone in the world right now? And can you do it quickly enough and effectively enough to keep up with whatever competition may arise? If not, you need to tap into resources to complement your team's expertise, so you can say yes to those questions.

As we've already mentioned, outsourcing tasks that others can do better can help you enhance the value you offer to your clients. But that isn't the only way. In many industries, new alliances are offering opportunities that never existed before to gain some of the advantages that come with scale. Teaming up with other business owners makes it possible to deliver greater value to your customers without working 24/7. Deciding to be the librarian, not the library, will unleash tremendous freedom to focus on what you do best.

Scott joined Carson Institutional Alliance, the group Ron started for elite financial advisors, to allow his firm to afford cutting-edge financial tools that would be too costly for his firm to develop on its own. By pooling his resources with other firms facing the same competitive pressures to deliver value, Scott can now prepare for a client meeting in thirty minutes (it used to take a full business day), or access research, updates, and trade notifications from his iPad, no matter where he happens to be. Instead of feeling worn out by the relentless challenge of delivering value, he is energized by working with members of the alliance who are constantly trying to do things better so all of their firms thrive.

Make sure that if you want to join an alliance, you vet it carefully to ensure that it will not only help you deliver more value to the people you serve but also connect you with other owners who energize you. When Scott began to consider joining an alliance, he wanted to improve his technology. But finding an alliance with a culture that complemented his own was even more important. He ultimately joined Carson Institutional Alliance, because he has so much in common with the other members. Alliance members have the same work ethic, for instance. Every morning, Scott's father would flip on Scott's light at 6:00 a.m. to do chores, whether it was a school day or not. This Midwestern work ethic made a strong impact on him. Scott felt an immediate kinship when he discovered that the members of the Carson Institutional Alliance all demonstrated the Midwestern work ethic he was so drawn to. It helps that they share personal passions, too. Members of the alliance are just as passionate about hunting as Scott is, for example. When you feel a genuine connection with the members of an alliance, you will feed off each other's energy and enthusiasm.

Joining an alliance isn't the only way to deliver more value to your customers. For some small firms, the answer lies in narrowing their niche even further in order to deliver the leading expertise in that area. Beyond joining Carson Institutional Alliance, Scott decided to focus even more closely on his ideal clients—entrepreneurs and business owners. To dominate that niche, he is strengthening his firm's service offerings in succession planning for business owners. If you do narrow your niche to a tightly focused specialty, make sure you mention it in your marketing. It will help you attract the ideal clients that contribute to the Sustainable Edge.

Make Your Value Clear

We live in a metrics-driven world. If you want to grow your business at 15 percent per year or more, clients need to see that you are delivering value for them, not just hear you talk about it. They must know without a doubt that you are moving the needle toward their goals. Otherwise, they may not fully understand what you are contributing and, as a result, may not continue to work with you. Our economy and world have evolved into a meritocracy. Both internally and externally, stakeholders increasingly hold each other accountable to deliver value. Don't kid yourself. There must be a visible exchange of value between you and your customers to hold onto them. You need to stand up and be measured—and want to be measured. Be prepared for the consequences if you are not delivering value. This will quickly become evident through your reporting. Customers will not stick with you if you are not moving the needle toward their goals. And if you are not delivering value, you will not survive.

So how do you deliver information in the right way? Once you have identified what matters to customers, you must create clear reporting tools to tell them about it. How do you know what information to provide and how frequently you should provide it? The answer is simple—client preference. Let the feedback you get from your client advisory council and other direct outreach guide you. Investing in access to the right technology will enable you to do so efficiently. In our industry, getting performance reporting right is a challenge for every firm, because of the complexities. Prior to joining Carson Institutional Alliance, Scott lost an A-plus client—something that has rarely happened at his firm—because a performance report was inaccurate and Scott could not explain why. It was a painful lesson, but he has learned from it and will not repeat it again.

Ron faced a similar challenge when he received an ultimatum from a $17 million client. The client said, "I'm going to give you one year to get your reporting to where it is at least as good as I can get by going to TD Ameritrade or Charles Schwab." It took Ron two and a half years to meet the challenge—but the client ultimately stuck with him. Ron knew he had succeeded in delivering value beyond a doubt when the client gave him candid feedback on the new client portal recently. Ron says, "Any time I am presented with a challenge, I have an opportunity to rise to that challenge to offer even greater service. If I get upset or frustrated by these challenges, I miss out on important growth opportunities."

Just as with key performance indicators, clear reporting tools will help you raise the bar on your own team's performance, because they make it impossible to hide. If you are not delivering value for clients, it will become clear very quickly. The good news is that if you learn how to use your own reporting tools in the best way possible, you will be able to pick up on weakness in your services before clients do—and fix them quickly.

"Any time I am presented with a challenge, I have an opportunity to rise to that challenge to offer even greater service. If I get upset or frustrated by these challenges, I miss out on important growth opportunities."

In the future, your industry will be disrupted. There is no doubt about that. Ask yourself some tough questions. Do you want to be the disrupted or the disruptor? Are you the Uber in your industry? If not, do you know how to acquire this status? If you don't figure this out, the disruptor will eventually put you out of business. Think of Ron's cab ride in Monaco. Can you imagine what will happen once Uber gains traction there? The driver who took Ron for a ride—both literally and figuratively—will be put out of business, because he will not do what Uber excels at, which is offering better service at a fraction of the cost. To deliver value without a doubt to your clients you must be the disruptor—not live in fear of it. That is the key to achieving the Sustainable Edge.

IQ Grower™ Exercises to Deliver Value Beyond a Doubt

Have you ever had reason to believe that any of your clients share in today's bias to distrust businesses in general or your firm in particular? If so, how can you combat that bias?

What steps can you take to confirm that you know exactly what your customers want?

What sort of advisory councils could you envision assembling in your particular industry? Think about councils that could be both informal and formal.

Who in your firm delivers results beyond the expected? Are they being compensated adequately for what they do? Does the thought of losing profit by increasing their compensation stand in the way of rewarding them? How can you resolve this dilemma?

Is your firm is missing a chance to deliver more value to your clients or customers, because you are bogged down in tasks that are not crucial to creating that value? If so, can you assign these tasks to entities outside your firm who specialize in them?

Is it perfectly clear to your customers that what you deliver is superior to that of your competitors? If not, do you have means in place to demonstrate the value of your firm to your customers beyond a shadow of a doubt?

What would a "disruptor" to your industry look like? Are you reaching out to, and immersing yourself in, groups that will provide the next inspiration for you to become such a disruptor?

Resource Link

Meritocracy:

http://www.inc.com/kip-tindell/how-to-make-your-business
-a-meritocracy.html

CONCLUSION:
PUT IT ALL TOGETHER

In the introduction, Scott faced the Ultimate Question. Ron asked him, "If you didn't wake up tomorrow, would your firm be the one you want managing your family's wealth?" You'll recall Scott's answer was, "Yes, but we could always do better."

Scott now has a very different answer to that question than he did when Ron first posed it. After committing to the IQ Grower™ process and focusing on the niche services he knows he can deliver, Scott is confident he has created the firm that he would want to manage his own family's wealth. He is certain he can compete with even the largest firms out there. He doesn't have any questions lingering at the back of his mind, nagging him about what he might do better. He is currently doing those things or working on achieving his goals with the members of Carson Institutional Alliance, Ron's alliance for elite advisors.

As a result of Scott's purposeful action to create the Sustainable Edge, he has achieved the freedom to enjoy time with the people who matter most to him right now, not ten years in the future when he finally becomes burned out from overwork. Although Scott is growing his firm more than 15 percent a year, he has had plenty of time to help his daughter, Lakin, launch her own business and share her own passion for entrepreneurship. To be able to pass on his life's passion to the next generation is worth more than anything to him.

Achieving the Sustainable Edge has helped deepen his life in immeasurable other ways, too. Scott's father was suffering from dementia near the end of his life. When Scott showed up at the nursing home after work for a visit one evening, he was dressed in the suit and tie he had worn to the office. "You sure look sharp. Where are you coming from?" his dad asked. "I was at work," Scott responded. Scott's dad looked him straight in the eye and asked with an unusual clarity, "Son, have you ever thought that if you worked as hard at God's kingdom or church as you do at work, just what impact that could possibly have and what good that could do?" That comment from his father stuck with him. Scott loves what he is doing, but he is intrigued by the possibilities it might suggest for his future. If he had not found the Sustainable Edge and created space in his life for the people who matter most to him, that conversation might never have happened. And like many hard-charging business owners, he wouldn't have been open to the value of it.

Ron, too, has achieved the Sustainable Edge, even while doing something that would seem to leave little time for anything else—running one of the twenty-five largest wealth management firms in the United States. Recently when an advisor donated to Ron's Dreamweaver Foundation, Ron invited him to his hunting lodge. Ron invited the advisor's wife, father, son, and brother-in-law to join them and really enjoyed seeing the wonderful family interact. Ron had also invited his own father and his sister. His father even brought his dog, so Ron had time to enjoy his own family, too. Ron savored the company and the weekend's hunting. An even better aspect was that Ron discovered the advisor, who manages $200 million in assets, was a good candidate for the client-centered approach of Carson Institutional Alliance.

The synergy of this weekend is a perfect example of Ron's emphasis on a Passion that Pays. Was it work? Was it play? It was neither, because it was both. When your work is your passion and your play is your passion, it is all just living.

Moments like these allow entrepreneurs to build their Sustainable Edge. Ron's passion and energy feeds his Passion that Pays—his work. His Passion that Pays, in turn, allows him to support his charity and pursue other things he enjoys. He enjoys the perfect virtuous cycle where it all feeds each other—the culmination of the lessons we have been sharing throughout the Sustainable Edge. Ron's weekend did not happen by accident, and we both enjoy synergy frequently in our lives, because we have set standards for ourselves. The standards we've set help us achieve the results we get. In short, taking purposeful action continues to feed the results we want.

It has been gratifying to see others achieve powerful results in their own lives using the IQ Grower™ system we have shared. When Robert Holdford joined Carson Institutional Alliance, his firm, Wealth Management in Little Rock, Arkansas, was only growing at about 5 to 7 percent a year. "We were at a point where my team said, 'We don't want to grow. We can't take on any more clients,'" Holdford recalls. "That wasn't something I was excited to hear from my team." After using the system we have outlined in this book to scale up, Holdford projected a growth of 30 to 40 percent in 2015. He and his partner, Brad Isroff, have teamed up with a third partner, who has about five hundred clients, and taken other steps. "We never would have considered being able to expand this way without the support of Carson Institutional Alliance and without Scott's coaching," says Holdford. "I spent my life wanting to make a difference in the world and believed [I] had reached the limit I was going to reach. Suddenly, overnight, I got to be part of this amazing organization. I'm very grateful." Meanwhile, Holdford's personal life has become immeasurably richer. A couple of months before we completed this book, Holdford remarried at the age of fifty. And, as talented electric guitarist, he still has time to play in the band at his church and in two cover bands. "I am grateful down to my molecules to be here and be able to live this life," he says.

To see if you're on track to achieving the Sustainable Edge, ask yourself some hard questions:

- Are you running the firm you would choose if money were no object and you could pick the best one there is?

- Knowing your business from the inside out, is your firm the one you would want to serve your family?

- And regardless of how well your firm is doing, are you leading a balanced life?

- Do you have plenty of free time to spend with the people who matter most to you and on the activities that energize you and help you make a difference?

- Are you taking care of your emotional, physical, and spiritual health—and not just plowing through a brutal to-do list every day?

Those are difficult and sometimes scary questions to answer. It is easy to gloss over them and just say yes, even if it is not true. But no matter what you say, your subconscious mind knows the truth. Business should not be your life. It should be a tool for you and others to get what you want out of your life. Ron's personal mission statement is to help others find more meaning and purpose in their lives. If we have freed you to do that, we will feel the book has been a success.

We also hope this book will give you time for reflection, meditation, and thought. That is what is missing in many of our lives today. We live in such a busy time that we don't really allow ourselves the space to make good decisions. Whether we are considering family decisions, work decisions, or health decisions, we are most often functioning on autopilot. Achieving the Sustainable Edge will give you the space to think more deeply and live your life on purpose, not by default.

While the client you met in the preface cannot undo the choices he made that led to where he is today, he still has time to move forward and build a life in which he is focused on what truly matters now. And so do you. Start turning things around today using the IQ Grower™ process, in conjunction with the strategies we have shared in these pages, to bring the Sustainable Edge to your business and your life. Begin by using the Essential Six and Most Vital exercises we outlined, and you will start to see results right away. Each of us has our own definition of having it all. Your definition may be very different from ours. But the tools for growing your business IQ and achieving the Sustainable Edge are the same for everyone:

- Tap into your subconscious.

- Find your niche.

- Call in reinforcements.

- Create your Brain Trust.

- Measure what matters.

- Live simply.

- Be vulnerable.

- Deliver value beyond a doubt.

Doing these takes some commitment on your part. There may be times when you find yourself slipping into old daily patterns wherein you find yourself busy without balance, or you have slipped and taken your eye off your firm's performance and find growth slowing. Events beyond your control, whether economic or personal, will always interfere with your best-laid plans. It happens to all of us. But the good news is that once you know our system, you can pick up where you left off and get right back on track at any time. Consider it your personal compass.

As Ron's client found, no matter how much success we achieve at work or how much wealth we build, we have only one life to live. Most members of our society may be on an unconscious journey to arrive at death safely, but you are free to drive your own destiny. The Sustainable Edge—what money can't buy and death can't take away—is available to everyone. The choice is yours. Will you live your life by design or by default? We hope that you'll use the strategies you've learned in this book to take charge of your life, instead of accepting what is handed to you, so that you can build your life around something that is truly special.

One of our favorite poems is "The Dash" by Linda Ellis (Copyright 1996). It often reminds us of the importance of creating space for what matters in our lives. We hope it will for you, too.

"The Dash" by Linda Ellis

I read of a man who stood to speak
at the funeral of a friend.
He referred to the dates on the tombstone
from the beginning . . . to the end.

He noted that first came the date of birth
and spoke the following date with tears,
but he said what mattered most of all
was the dash between those years.

For that dash represents all the time
that they spent alive on earth.
And now only those who loved them
know what that little line is worth.

For it matters not, how much we own,
the cars . . . the house . . . the cash.
What matters is how we live and love
and how we spend our dash.

So, think about this long and hard.
Are there things you'd like to change?
For you never know how much time is left
that can still be rearranged.

If we could just slow down enough
to consider what's true and real
and always try to understand
the way other people feel.
And be less quick to anger
and show appreciation more
and love the people in our lives
like we've never loved before.

If we treat each other with respect
and more often wear a smile,
remembering that this special dash
might only last a little while.

So, when your eulogy is being read,
with your life's actions to rehash . . .
would you be proud of the things they say
about how you spent YOUR dash?

IQ GROWER™ PROCESS CHART

IQ Grower™ Process: Daily

Do this before leaving the office or before going to bed.

---

1 WHAT IS MY ATTITUDE OF GRATITUDE?

List 3 things you are grateful for today and 3 things you hope to be grateful for tomorrow.

Today	Tomorrow
1. _____	1. _____
2. _____	2. _____
3. _____	3. _____

---

2 WHAT ACTIVITIES DRIVE MY QUARTERLY GOALS/PRIORITIES?

List your number 1 thing to accomplish for tomorrow,
then list the 6 most important thin to accomplish tomorrow in priority order.

Vital 1	How Good (HG) 1–10	How Excited (HE) 1–10

6 Most		
Goals	(HG) 1–10	(HE) 1–10

IQ Grower™ Process: Quarterly

Do this every 3 months.
What you value may not change, but priorities and goals for the quarter will.

---

1 **WHAT I VALUE MOST & WHAT IS THE MOST MEANINGFUL TO ME?**

List in order of priority the things you value most and are most meaningful to you.

1. _____   4. _____

2. _____   5. _____

3. _____   6. _____

---

2 **BHAG "BIG HAIRY AUDACIOUS GOAL" FROM JIM COLLINS**

List your 6 most important goals for 10-25 years from now.

1. _____   4. _____

2. _____   5. _____

3. _____   6. _____

---

3 **WHAT ARE MY GOALS FOR THIS QUARTER THAT WILL MOVE ME IN THE DIRECTION OF MY BHAG?**

When you are finished, pick the most important of the 6 goals to focus on for the quarter and circle it.

1. _____   4. _____

2. _____   5. _____

3. _____   6. _____

APPENDIX B:
BLUEPRINTING PROCESS WORKSHEET

Blueprinting—Find Your "Why"

The Blueprinting process is a series of exercises we created to help you live your life by design, not by default. The purpose of these exercises is to help ignite your relentless burning desire and lead you to personal fulfillment. In other words, it will help you find your Why.

This series of six exercises will help you develop a crystal clear map of where you want to go personally and what you want to accomplish professionally. As a result, the new clarity gained will help make your life much more meaningful and your business much more profitable.

Completing the Blueprinting exercises is the key to igniting your relentless burning desire. Igniting this desire requires you to dig deep. You have to spend some serious time reflecting, contemplating, and being authentic with yourself. This is not something you're going to knock out in a weekend. It could take weeks, or even months, before it fully evolves into a clear picture of your future.

Values | Step #1—Identify What You Value Most

All people have certain principles and values they believe in and live by. These are the innermost beliefs that distinguish who we are and how we conduct ourselves. Values are things that are very important to us. They include such aspects of life as family, health, career, and spirituality. Having strong convictions about what we value and keeping them front and center in our lives keeps us balanced and focused on the most important things. In the long run, focusing on what you value, coupled with solid principles, will help you live a fulfilling life that is far more satisfying than any short-term gain from compromising.

Having these strong convictions benefits you in other ways, too. In times of indecision, you can turn to your guiding values. They will frequently give you the framework for making tough decisions. When you're unhappy, you can turn to your values and see if you're leading a life that is consistent with your beliefs. When you're under-achieving, you can turn to your values and gain the motivation to make the extra effort.

DECISION MAKING:

Have you ever had trouble making a decision? In business and in life, we have to make decisions all the time. Many of them involve "gray" areas where more than one solution will work. Indecisiveness results when you are not clear on your values. Once you bring clarity to your values, making decisions becomes easy.

HAPPINESS:

Far too many people in our society go through life without zest and enthusiasm. Frequently, this is because they are doing things and being things that are not congruent with who they are. The result can be burnout, depression, and ineffectiveness. The key is to check what is important to you and then make sure your life is in sync with that.

ACHIEVEMENT:

Some of the greatest fulfillment in life has come from people who felt so strongly in their values that they were willing to devote their lives, and in some cases, sacrifice their lives, to live them. The key is to feel so strongly about your values that you are motivated to take action and live by them. Having conviction about something you value, and then committing to living by it every single day, will go a long way toward igniting your relentless burning desire.

Values | Step #1–Identify What You Value Most

In this exercise, you'll identify what you value most in life and then rank them from most important to least important. Examples that might appear on your list include:

Family · Health · Spiritual Fulfillment · Love · Relationships Generosity · Adventure · Achievement · Passion · Creativity · Leaving a Legacy · Fun/Happiness · Positive Attitude · Learning · Helping Others · Simplicity · Financial Security · Peace of Mind · Respect Gratitude · Abundance · Compassion · Faith · Growth · Honesty Integrity · Kindness · Selflessness · Significance · Vitality · Wisdom Intimacy · Security · Peace

DIRECTIONS:

List at least six things you value most in life and then rank them in order of importance. Then, indicate the actual percentage of time you spend living and supporting these values.

THE THINGS I VALUE MOST IN LIFE ARE:

Value	Rank	% of Time

Values | Step #1—Identify What You Value Most

Take a close look at your list. Are you spending a lot of time living and supporting your values?

Remember: Values are not some fluffy ideal. They need to be fundamental to who you are as a human being. With that said, some of your values may change over time due to changing circumstances in your life. What's important to you today may not be as important to you five years from now. Consequently, it's important to review your values on a regular basis to make sure they are still important to you.

To get more focused on your values, restate your top six values in the chart below, then list one key action you can implement that will help you more fully integrate that value into your life. For example, let's say health is one of your top six values. Here's how that line on the chart might look:

Value	Action to Integrate It More Fully into My Life
1. Health	Exercise at least 30 minutes a day, 5 days a week

Now complete the full chart:

Value	Action to Integrate It More Fully into My Life
1.	
2.	
3.	

4.	
5.	
6.	

You'll refer to this chart a little later as you work on developing your goals. Long term, to keep your values top of mind, review this list on a regular basis.

Purpose | Step #2–Find Your Meaningful Purpose

We all have certain desires and pursuits in life, such as ensuring our security and caring for loved ones. But, when we move beyond the day-to-day pursuits of life, what moves you? What causes you to jump out of bed in the morning feeling refreshed and ready to tackle the day's challenges? What higher purpose calls you? What is something larger than yourself that inspires you? What can you do that uses all your skills, talents, and interests, and that benefits the world?

Without meaningful purpose, we simply go through the motions of life. We respond to the alarm clock, we go to work, we solve the day's problems, we eat, we relax, we spend a few minutes with the family, we go to bed, and then we wake up and do it all over again. We could do that for fifty years and then look back on what we've accomplished and be sadly disappointed at how much time we spent accomplishing so little. Each of us is capable of making a very positive impact in the life we live.

For many people, being a loving spouse and raising great kids is a huge accomplishment, and they should be rightfully proud of that. Meaningful purpose goes a step beyond and transcends what we do for ourselves and our immediate family. Meaningful purpose reaches out to the world around us and infuses life with the special gifts that each of us have inside.

Purpose | Step #2—Find Your Meaningful Purpose

The following exercise is designed to help you identify, unlock, and pursue your meaningful purpose, so the world can benefit from your unique gifts. Following are a series of questions. Your objective is to reflect on them, write your response, and then consciously decide how you are going to move forward living your life with meaningful purpose.

1. Are you committed to finding your meaningful purpose in life and, if so, what has happened in your life that makes you ready? _____

_____

_____

_____

2. What are your unique gifts? In other words, what do you do extremely well? _____

    _____

    _____

    _____

3. What do you most value in life? (Restate your top values from Step #1.) _____

    _____

    _____

    _____

4. What activities are you most passionate about? For example, what gives you a great feeling of satisfaction and fulfillment?

    _____

    _____

    _____

    _____

5. What social issues are you so passionate about that you would write an editorial in your local newspaper advocating your position? _____

    _____

    _____

    _____

6. Given a choice, do you prefer to help people by rolling up your sleeves and pitching in, or do you prefer a more

behind-the-scenes role? Give examples of the types of activities you like to do based on your response. _____

_____

_____

7. When you feel empty and directionless in life, what is missing in your life during those times that is causing you to feel that way? _____

_____

_____

_____

8. How are you nourishing your soul spiritually? _____

_____

_____

_____

9. Is your spouse/significant other supportive in your desire to more fully live your meaningful purpose? If not, how are you reconciling that? _____

_____

_____

_____

10. How do you go about making an important decision about your life direction? Is it made from a surface level, or do

you have a way of checking into your soul? Do you have a confidant who can help guide you? _____

_____

_____

_____

11. Do you view a lack of money as an impediment to fully realizing your meaningful purpose? If so, what are some creative ways that you can get past this issue? _____

_____

_____

_____

12. If you live your life with meaningful purpose, how will the world be a better place? _____

_____

_____

_____

13. How will you know that you are living your life with meaningful purpose? _____

_____

_____

_____

14. Based on your answers to the previous questions, take some time now to jot down your thoughts on what your purpose in life may be. Granted, this is a tall order, but you have to

start somewhere. Make some notes, then set it aside for a while and let it sink in. Revisit what you wrote and see if it still feels congruent. Continue this process until you come to that "aha" moment, and you know you've got it! _____

_____

_____

_____

Meaningful Purpose Notes

_____

_____

_____

Vision | Step #3–Create a Compelling Vision of Your Future

There's an old saying, "If you don't know where you're going, any road will get you there." That's a recipe for mediocrity. People of great achievement know exactly where they're going, and they take the necessary steps to get there. But, where is "there" for you?

"There" is your ideal future scenario. This is the dream life and dream business you would create if you had absolutely no constraints and could simply wave a magic wand and make it happen. It's your vision for your environmental surroundings, the people you associate with, what you spend your time doing, and what you want to accomplish. It's different for everybody. For example, perhaps you want to be successfully self-employed, working from home, and living in the mountains. Or, perhaps you want to work for a nonprofit organization that speaks to your heart and live near your children and grandchildren. It can be anything, but it must be something, and it must be clearly defined. It must include tangibles, so you can see it, feel it, touch it, smell it, and hear it to get all your senses involved in helping you drive toward it.

Your vision must be compelling. It must be something that motivates you to jump out of bed in the morning and get working. Your vision is what will sustain you when the going gets tough and you face major obstacles. To develop it, disengage from the present and position yourself in a future with unlimited possibilities. Eliminate your limiting beliefs and think big. With this frame of mind, you can develop a vision that propels you to success, contribution, and happiness far beyond what you've ever imagined. The key to your compelling vision is to create one that motivates you to take action and that helps you persevere even when times are difficult. Here's an example of a compelling vision of the future:

> I enthusiastically jump out of bed every morning full of love for God, family, friends, and life. I am a husband my wife is proud of, a father my children look up to, and a friend people count on. My family is financially secure, physically fit, and emotionally close. We live in a comfortable home

on one acre with a postcard-perfect view of the Pacific Ocean. Our home is light and airy with crisp ocean breezes blowing through. Pictures of my family and special moments in our life line the walls. The sound of grandchildren fills the house. As I look out the window, I see waves lapping the shore, seals playing on the rocks, and surfers hanging ten.

My days are spent helping the people around me reach their fullest potential. I do this by meeting with my top clients, guiding them in reaching their dreams and aspirations, and communicating my wisdom through my life planning website. My financial success enables me to be a reverse tither, and I give away 90 percent of my income and live on 10 percent. My schedule is flexible, and I spend several hours a week mentoring disadvantaged children. For recreation, my wife and I travel the world, visit our kids and grandkids, read, and take time to enjoy the beauty of the great outdoors. When I go to bed at night, I sleep soundly knowing that I helped make the world a little better than it was when I woke up.

Vision | Step #3—Create a Compelling Vision of Your Future

In this exercise, you'll paint a picture of your compelling vision.

DIRECTIONS:

Don't hold back. Finish each statement as accurately and completely as possible. This is your future, so make it a great one!

1. My ideal working environment is . . . _____

_____

_____

2. The relationships I want to surround myself with include . . .

_____

_____

3. I want to spend my days working on . . . _____

_____

_____

4. If I weren't so afraid, I would . . . _____

_____

_____

5. My life will not be complete unless I . . . _____

_____

_____

6. If I knew for certain that I would die peacefully in either fourteen days or fourteen weeks (and I didn't know which of these two dates I would die), I would do the following in the next fourteen days . . . _____

_____

_____

7. And I would do the following in the remaining twelve weeks (assuming I live that long) . . . _____

_____

_____

8. If I had all the money I ever needed, I would spend the rest of my life . . . _____

_____

_____

9. I want people to remember me by saying I was . . . _____

_____

_____

10. My most memorable experiences include . . . _____

_____

_____

11. The part of my weekly routine that I look forward to is . . .

_____

_____

12. I feel alive and energetic after I have just . . . _____

_____

_____

13. The community/world issue that I feel most strongly about is . . . _____

_____

14. It may seem impossible today, but my life would dramatically improve if . . . _____

_____

_____

Vision | Step #3—Create a Compelling Vision of Your Future

Review how you finished all the previous statements. From this, use the following outline to write a compelling vision that motivates you to take action and that gives you great excitement just thinking about it.

MY COMPELLING VISION IS TO . . .

Remember to include whom you'd like to surround yourself with, where you'd like to live, how you'd like to spend your days, and what you'd like to accomplish.

Once you create a compelling vision that gives you goose bumps, review it on a daily basis to continue hardwiring it into your life, so it will keep inspiring you.

Faith & Success | Step #4—Develop a Personal and Professional Mission Statement

A mission statement is not simply a hokey statement that gets written once and then filed away. Rather, it is a living, breathing document that should be displayed prominently for visual reinforcement and internalized to keep your subconscious working on it. Spend time developing it, memorizing it, and living it, and you'll be pleasantly surprised at the results.

Faith | Step #4—Develop a Personal Mission Statement

Creating a personal mission statement will be one of the most important things you do in your life. Therefore, please set aside some time for reflection to complete it. It will evolve over time, but it is important to get a draft on paper, so you can continue to shape it.

A personal mission statement is a bold statement about the kind of life you want to lead, who you want to be, and how you want to conduct yourself. It will serve as your lighthouse during difficult times and keep you motivated, focused, and true throughout your life. Share it with your spouse or significant other.

HERE'S AN EXAMPLE OF A PERSONAL MISSION STATEMENT:

My mission is to be loving and loyal to my family and friends, lead a successful career that I enjoy, stay healthy, and take on any challenges that come my way.

I value my family, friends, spiritual fulfillment, sense of accomplishment, and enthusiasm. I value my relationship with God and live by the Golden Rule.

Throughout my life, I will always be supportive and loyal to my family and friends. I will be an active member in my place of worship and in my local community. I will use my financial management skills to help needy organizations keep their financial houses in order.

I will live life to the fullest and strongly believe that nothing is impossible.

Your personal mission statement may follow a similar format or you may want to modify it. The key is to make it personal, meaningful, and inspirational.

Faith | Step #4—Develop a Personal Mission Statement

In this exercise, you'll create a personal mission statement.

A personal mission statement is your declaration of the kind of person you want to be. It answers such questions as: Who do I want to be? How do I conduct myself? What and who are important to me? Think of it as a daily guide to living.

DIRECTIONS:

Take some time to write a draft of your personal mission statement. The key is to get something down on paper. Let it percolate and then come back to it. Eventually, solidify and review it each day.

Personal Mission Statement

_____

_____

_____

Success | Step #4—Develop a Professional Mission Statement

Your professional mission statement is your business guide. It can address such issues as who you are, why you exist, whom you serve, and what results your clients can expect. After you develop it, share it with your team and your clients. Let it permeate your office and guide you and your team's actions.

HERE ARE SEVERAL EXAMPLES OF PROFESSIONAL MISSION STATEMENTS SUBMITTED BY FINANCIAL ADVISORS:

To create a world of financial comfort by implementing custom solutions to individual needs!

We are dedicated to enhancing the quality of our clients' lives as we oversee their wealth to help them achieve their long-term goals and dreams. With our unmatched superior service and guidance, we build strong relationships as we help simplify our clients' financial affairs. This enables them to focus on those areas that give their life meaning and purpose.

To guide our clients through the process of obtaining financial peace of mind, so they can focus on the most important things in life.

To guide our clients in making wise decisions based on Biblical principles for wealth management.

Similar to a personal mission statement, make it personal, meaningful, and inspirational. Both statements should be reasonably short and highly memorable. There's no set length to a mission statement. Just make sure you can remember it and that it connects with you.

Success | Step #4–Develop a Professional Mission Statement

In this exercise, you'll create a professional mission statement.

A professional mission statement is your declaration of the kind of business/career you want to have. It answers such questions as: What does my firm do? How do we do it? Why do we exist? What can our clients expect? If you are an employee, and not a business owner, write it from the perspective of how you do your job.

DIRECTIONS:

Take some time to write a draft of your professional mission statement. The key is to get something down on paper. Let it percolate and then come back to it. Eventually, solidify and review it each day.

Professional Mission Statement

_____

_____

_____

Define | Step #5—Express Your Value

A value proposition defines what makes your practice unique and the experience to be delivered to your clients. A simple way to create a value proposition is to select key words from your professional mission statement and define each key word to answer why a prospect should do business with you or what the experience will be when the prospect is a client.

CREATE YOUR PROFESSIONAL MISSION STATEMENT.

Your professional mission statement should be one sentence long and address the following three questions:

1. Who are you and what makes you different? _____

   _____

   _____

   _____

2. What do you actually do for your clients? _____

   _____

   _____

   _____

3. How do you do it? _____

   _____

   _____

Professional Mission Statement

Rewrite your professional mission statement here.

_____

_____

_____

Define | Step #5 – Express Your Value

SAMPLE VALUE PROPOSITION FROM CARSON WEALTH MANAGEMENT GROUP

You are here today to decide if there is a compelling reason for you to work with me and my practice. The mission statement at Carson Wealth Management Group is:

> To **inspire** our clients in making **informed decisions** through **education, communication,** and **service that exceeds their expectations.**

Our mission statement is more than just words; it's the action we take. Let me define for you what a few of the key words in our mission statement mean to me.

- **Inspire:** Our goal is to inspire you, our client, to live your life by design, not by default. Money is a tool to get the most out of your life.

- **Informed Decisions:** Once you are inspired to share what you want out of life, we help you make informed decisions that are logical for you. Our skilled Certified Financial Planner, CPA, Attorney, and Insurance Specialist bring our resources together to develop a plan, so you can accomplish your dreams.

- **Education:** Making informed decisions can only be accomplished by providing you with some education. You don't need to understand everything we are doing, but you do need a 10,000-foot view of what we are doing, why we are doing it, and how it applies to you.

- **Communication:** Our communication doesn't stop at education. Many firms claim to communicate frequently with clients, but we take it a step further and we over-communicate, so you know we know you as a person and not just an account. You will never be disappointed in the level of communication you receive from Carson Wealth Management Group.

- **Service That Exceeds Your Expectations:** We deliver a level of service that will exceed your expectations. In our country, expectation of service has never been lower. So, we are going in a different direction. We provide a Four Seasons experience with FedEx efficiency.

How can we do all this? We are independent and sit on the same side of the table as you. We have a seamless proactive service process that simply means we anticipate your needs before you even know there is a need. It means being bifocal, which means paying attention to what is happening today and anticipating changes on the horizon. Additionally, the entire team does their piece to add value to the process, which means it's not about working with Ron Carson, but about having a systemized approach so you get to:

Experience the Carson Wealth Way

Does this sound like the type of relationship you are looking for from the company managing your wealth?

Define | Step #5–Express Your Value

CREATE YOUR VALUE PROPOSITION

After you have a solid mission statement, the value proposition can be created. In your previous mission statement, highlight three to five key words you can define for your clients and prospects to answer the following questions:

1. Why should I do business with you? _____

   _____

   _____

   _____

2. What will my experience be like working with you? _____

_____

_____

_____

3. Keyword or Phrase #1:
   Define: _____

_____

_____

_____

4. Key Word or Phrase #2:
   Define: _____

_____

_____

_____

5. Key Word or Phrase #3:
   Define: _____

_____

_____

_____

6. Key Word or Phrase #4:
   Define: _____

_____

_____

_____

7. Key Word or Phrase #5:

Define: _____

_____

_____

_____

Define | Step #5—Express Your Value

PUT IT ALL TOGETHER!

Create a story, drawing together your key words from your mission statement, ending with a "punch line," connecting it all together.

Your Value Proposition

_____

_____

_____

Dream | Step #6—Set One-, Three-, Five-, and Ten-Year Goals

We all have wants and desires. We all daydream about what it would be like to be living our ideal life. Unfortunately, merely thinking about our ideal life will not get us our ideal life. We have to be clear about what we want, when we want it, and why we want it. We also have to take positive action to make it happen. The goal-setting process is critical to making all of this happen. As we set goals, make sure they are SMAC-certified—Specific, Measurable, Achievable, and Compatible.

One of the keys to goal-setting is to tie them into your compelling vision. Your compelling vision is a lifetime pursuit. To make that manageable, you have to break it into pieces. To do this, complete the goal-setting and action-planning exercises. As you set goals, start by reviewing your compelling vision and then work backward. To pursue your vision, what has to happen in ten years, five years, three years, and one year? Determine what age you, your spouse, and your children will be at each of those time periods. Identify the goal, then determine the one activity that will have the greatest impact on reaching that goal. Also, identify the reward you will get by reaching the goal.

Here are examples of categories in which you might want to set goals:

- **Attitude:** Are there any attitudes or limiting beliefs you need to change in order to reach your compelling vision?

- **Career:** What do you want to accomplish in your professional life?

- **Education:** Do you need additional knowledge that will help you pursue your vision?

- **Family:** How can you improve your relationships?

- **Financial:** What net worth are you striving for? What business financial goals do you have?

- **Physical:** What specific physical goals can you set? Do you want to be a certain weight? Do you want to exercise a certain amount? Is there a challenging physical goal you'd like to achieve such as climbing Mount Rainier?

- **Recreation:** What do you want to do in your free time that will rejuvenate you?

- **Community:** What do you want to do for your community? What legacy do you want to leave?

- **Spiritual:** How do you want to grow in your spirituality?

Once you've set your goals, transfer them to the Visualize and Realize section at the very end of this process. This will neatly summarize your compelling vision and all the activities that have to take place to make it happen.

Dream | Step #6—Set One-, Three-, Five-, and Ten-Year Goals

SAMPLE: ONE-YEAR GOALS

GOAL	KEY ACTIVITY TO ACHIEVE	REWARD
Change my belief system from scarcity to abundance	Read appropriate books and listen to the right speakers and take them to heart	A better outlook on life
Take a two-week family vacation	Schedule it	Grow closer as a family, smiling faces, new experiences
Exercise vigorously at least five days per week	Join the local health club, get up by 5:15 a.m., hire a personal trainer for six months	Great health, feel good, more energy
Break 80 in golf	Practice more and focus on eliminating double bogies	New set of clubs
Become a member of the leadership team at my place of worship	Express my desire and follow the protocol to obtain the position	Being able to help people
Meditate at least fifteen minutes a day	Find a consistent time that works and create a peaceful space	Stress reduction, clear mind, greater understanding
Spend five hours per week helping kids with homework or as much time as needed	Let kids know I'm available and make it a priority	Smarter, happier kids, satisfaction from helping, grow closer to the kids

DIRECTIONS:

On the following pages, write down your goals for the next one-, three-, five-, and ten-year periods. After that, transfer the goals that relate to you achieving your compelling vision on the Visualize and Realize page.

Dream | Step #6—Set One-, Three-, Five-, and Ten-Year Goals

ONE-YEAR GOALS

My Age: _____   Spouse's Age: _____   Kids' Ages: _____

GOAL	KEY ACTIVITY TO ACHIEVE	REWARD

THREE-YEAR GOALS

My Age: _____   Spouse's Age: _____   Kids' Ages: _____

GOAL	KEY ACTIVITY TO ACHIEVE	REWARD

FIVE-YEAR GOALS

My Age: _____   Spouse's Age: _____   Kids' Ages: _____

GOAL	KEY ACTIVITY TO ACHIEVE	REWARD

TEN-YEAR GOALS

My Age: _____   Spouse's Age: _____   Kids' Ages: _____

GOAL	KEY ACTIVITY TO ACHIEVE	REWARD

VISUALIZE AND REALIZE

Year One Goals

_____

_____

_____

Year Three Goals

_____

_____

_____

Year Five Goals

_____

_____

_____

Year Ten Goals

_____

_____

_____

APPENDIX C:

SAMPLE QUARTERLY DASHBOARD

Quarterly Dashboard: Our 13-Week Race Results

Quarterly Goals

	Accountable Member	Q1 2009	Green	Yellow	Red	Week 1	Week 2
1							
2							
3							
4							
5							
6							
7							
8							
9							
10							

Quarterly Priorities

	Priority	Who/When		Green	Yellow	Red	Week 1	Week 2
1								
2								
3								
4								
5								

Quarterly Critical Numbers

	Accountable Member	Q1 2009	Green	Yellow	Red	Week 1	Week 2
1		Productivity Metric					
2		People Metric					

Week 5	Week 6	Week 7	Week 8	Week 9	Week 10	Week 11	Week 12	Week 13

Week 5	Week 6	Week 7	Week 8	Week 9	Week 10	Week 11	Week 12	Week 13

Week 5	Week 6	Week 7	Week 8	Week 9	Week 10	Week 11	Week 12	Week 13

APPENDIX D:

RESOURCES

Chapter 1

Carson Institutional Alliance
http://www.carsoninstitutional.com/

Peak Advisor Alliance
http://peakadvisoralliance.com

Carson Wealth Management Group
http://www.carsonwealth.com/
rcarson@carsonwealth.com

Cornerstone Wealth Management Group
http://www.cornerstonewealthgroup.com/
scottf@cornerstonewealthgroup.com

Steve Jobs Stanford Commencement Speech, June 2005
http://www.ted.com/talks/steve_jobs_how_to_live_before_you_die

Managing Your Energy for Productivity
http://www.actionablebooks.com/en-ca/summaries
/be-excellent-at-anything/

Energy Champion Resource Kit (The Energy Project/Tony Schwartz)
http://theenergyproject.com/landing/energy-champion

Chapter 2

Identify Your Why
www.startwithwhy.com

Chapter 3

Identifying and Developing Strengths

http://www.strengthsfinder.com

http://www.gallup.com/businessjournal/102310
/CliftonStrengthFinder-Book-Center.aspx

Now Discover Your Strengths, **Clifton, PhD, Donald O.**

https://hbr.org/2012/08/the-disciplined-pursuit-of-less

Learning to Say No

http://zenhabits.net/say-no/

Asking for Feedback—Customer Advisory Board Best Practices

http://www.customeradvisoryboard.org

How to Ensure Your Feedback Program Doesn't Fail

http://www.forbes.com/sites/ericjackson/2012/08/17
/the-7-reasons-why-360-degree-feedback-programs-fail/

Chapter 4

https://www.gazelles.com/static/resources/tools/en/growth-tools-all.pdf

http://www.theceoadvantage.com/resources/quarterly-rocks.html

SWOT Analysis

http://www.quickmba.com/strategy/swot/

Chapter 5

Crowdsourcing
https://hbr.org/2013/04/using-the-crowd-as-an-innovation-partner/

How to Build a Brain Trust
http://www.lifehack.org/articles/productivity
/how-to-start-and-run-a-mastermind-group.html

Gazelles
https://www.gazelles.com/

**Using LinkedIn for Your Brain Trust/Searching LinkedIn
for Mastermind Groups**
https://www.linkedin.com/grp/

Chapter 6

http://kpilibrary.com/
https://www.gazelles.com/static/resources/tools/en/growth-tools-all.pdf

Metrics That Give You an Edge—Examples of KPIs
www.kpilibrary.com

Understanding Leading vs. Lagging Indicators—Doctor vs. Coroner
http://www.projecttimes.com/articles/lagging-vs.-leading-business
-indicators-do-you-know-the-difference.html

Chapter 7

TED Talk

http://www.ted.com/talks/graham_hill_less_stuff_more_happiness

Chapter 8

The Value of Vulnerability with Patrick Lencioni
https://www.youtube.com/watch?v=MIobVupCCto

On Being Boldly Vulnerable—the Book *Daring Greatly*
by Brene Brown
Her TED Talk on Vulnerability: http://www.ted.com/talks
/brene_brown_on_vulnerability?language=en
www.brenebrown.com

On Vulnerability, 360-Degree Feedback, Truth-Giving and
Receiving—the Book What Got You Here Won't Get You There
by Marshall Goldsmith
http://www.marshallgoldsmithlibrary.com

USD Talk on YouTube
https://www.youtube.com/watch?v=xY7UJVYM9n0&safe=active

More about Meditation/Mindfulness
www.relaxationresponse.org/steps

Chapter 9

http://www.inc.com/kip-tindell/how-to-make-your-business
-a-meritocracy.html

ABOUT THE AUTHORS

Ron Carson is the founder and CEO of Carson Wealth, one of the largest wealth advisory firms in the country, serving clients through holistic financial planning, disciplined investment strategies, and proactive personal service. He is one of the most celebrated and respected financial advisors and executives in the industry and is a sought after speaker, thinker, and investment strategist. Ron has shared his success principles, as documented in his book, *Tested in the Trenches*, with audiences worldwide. Most recently, Ron coauthored *The New York Times* best-selling book *Avalanche* and the Blueprinting process that goes with it. Together, these tools help advisors learn how to clarify their mission, vision, and values by setting business and life goals. Ron and his wife, Jeanie, reside in

Omaha, Nebraska. They have three wonderful children, two dogs, and a cat. Ron enjoys spending time with his family, golfing, flying, and pheasant hunting.

Scott Ford, founder and CEO of Cornerstone Wealth Management Group and a Carson Institutional partner, serves on the investment committee as the technical strategist. He is a registered principal at LPL Financial and is a registered financial consultant. Scott is ranked in the top 1 percent of all LPL registered financial advisors based on annual production. He was recognized as one of the 20 Rising Stars of Wealth Management by *Private Asset Management Magazine*[1]. Scott is the author of two books: *Financial Jiu-Jitsu: A Fighter's Guide to Conquering Your Finances* and *The Widow's Wealth Map: Six Steps to Beginning Again*. Scott and his wife, Angie, reside in Hagerstown, Maryland, and have two children, a dog, and a cat. In addition to spending time with his family and church, Scott enjoys golf, hunting, and Brazilian Jiu-Jitsu.

Securities offered through LPL Financial, Member FINRA/ SIPC. Investment advisory services offered through CWM, LLC, a Registered Investment Advisor. LPL Financial is under separate ownership from any other named entity.

---

1. *Institutional Investor News'* "The 20 Rising Stars of Wealth Management" is based on nominations submitted by investment management professionals, selected by publishing staff. Award criteria is based on $1 million dollars in investable assets per private client and demonstrating strong relationship and portfolio skills.